Understand Need / Segment

Needs
- listen to customers
- Customer Case Research. Interview ~~~~~~~~~~~~ Product
- Word of mouth : - connectors : people with a lot of connections
    - Mavens : information broker. that gives credibility to the message
    - Salesmen : the one. that persuade others of the message

- Market surveys are good but not as good as knowing at what C do

Segment
- Successful. Cie : x design the right off to the customer.
    x focus the entire company to the offer.
    x develop capability. to improve.

- Customer :   profit   high
                                     Low.

- adduct errors   default promote

- Custom data : global/aggregated / interviews / Individual data point

The Results-Driven Manager Series

The Results-Driven Manager series collects timely articles from *Harvard Management Update*, *Harvard Management Communication Letter*, and the *Balanced Scorecard Report* to help senior to middle managers sharpen their skills, increase their effectiveness, and gain a competitive edge. Presented in a concise, accessible format to save managers valuable time, these books offer authoritative insights and techniques for improving job performance and achieving immediate results.

Other books in the series:

Teams That Click

Presentations That Persuade and Motivate

Face-to-Face Communications for Clarity and Impact

Winning Negotiations That Preserve Relationships

Managing Yourself for the Career You Want

Getting People on Board

Taking Control of Your Time

Dealing with Difficult People

Managing Change to Reduce Resistance

Becoming an Effective Leader

Motivating People for Improved Performance

Hiring Smart for Competitive Advantage

Retaining Your Best People

A Timesaving Guide

THE RESULTS-DRIVEN MANAGER

Connecting with Your Customers

• • •

Harvard Business School Press

Boston, Massachusetts

Library of Congress Cataloging-in-Publication Data

Connecting with your customers
        p. cm. — (The results-driven manager series)
    ISBN 10 1-4221-0323-4
    ISBN 13 978-1-4221-0323-4
  1. Customer relations. 2. Customer services. 3. Success in business.
I. Harvard Business School. II. Series.
    HF5415.5.C658 2006
    658.8'12—dc22

                                            2006007913

Contents

Contents

Enhancing Customer Loyalty

Introduction

. . .

Do you manage a customer service group? Lead a team in the accounting or purchasing department? Manage a human resources or public relations group? Head up a product line or brand? Play a supervisory role in the logistics or information technology unit? No matter where you work in your company, you can get to know your firm's customers better—and generate valuable results for the organization as well as enhance your own standing. When you understand customers' needs and preferences, you can more effectively support your company's efforts to delight customers and win their loyalty—which translates into greater profits for your firm.

If you work in sales, marketing, customer service, or product development, the connection between your everyday activities and your firm's customers is obvious. It's clear that you need a comprehensive understanding of customers' preferences in order to develop savvy sales strategies, create marketing campaigns that appeal to target segments, resolve customers' concerns promptly, or design products and services that will score major successes in the marketplace. And if you work in other parts of the organization, where the connection to customers isn't so clear, it's equally vital that you get to know your firm's customers. By doing so, you can generate fresh ideas for better meeting their needs. For instance:

- A supply chain manager learns that customers are expecting faster-than-ever delivery times. She forges partnerships with new distribution channel partners to accelerate delivery of her company's products.

- An accounting manager reads an article citing consumers' growing frustration with invoice errors and their tendency to defect to competing companies when error rates increase. He establishes a new process for reducing invoicing errors.

- An IT manager discovers that visitors to company Web sites spend more if navigation around the sites is simple and quick. She redesigns her firm's site so that first-time visitors who want to make a purchase are asked to provide their name, address, and credit-card information only once.

- A purchasing manager knows that his company's customers are becoming more price sensitive. He negotiates more favorable agreements with suppliers so his company can pass savings along to customers in the form of lower prices.

When managers throughout a company take responsibility for understanding and better serving customers, they generate measurable results for their firm. Perhaps most important, satisfied customers stay loyal to your company and tell their friends and acquaintances about their experiences with your firm. Loyalty and positive word of mouth save your company the steep cost of acquiring new customers and thereby boost profitability. Delighted customers also spend more and sample more of your company's offerings, increasing cash flow and market share. And they may be more open to helping your organization design successful products and services by participating in focus groups and other research activities.

Understanding your company's customers also enables you to communicate with them in mutually beneficial ways—whether through formal marketing campaigns, sales presentations, or informal encounters via phone or e-mail. And it helps you further enhance customer loyalty by addressing the reasons behind defections and ensuring that first-time buyers are transformed into repeat business.

Yet despite these potential rewards, getting to know

your company's customers is challenging—and getting more so every day. As new technologies and product possibilities have reshaped markets, many firms are finding it increasingly difficult to pin down what consumers want, how their wishes and needs will change in the short and long run, and what will keep them loyal. Moreover, in this age of information, the balance of power has shifted away from companies and toward consumers: using the Internet, everyday shoppers can now easily access reviews of competing firms' offerings and quickly compare prices and product specifications. The implication? Traditional smoke-and-mirrors marketing campaigns do not work anymore: today's firms must truly understand consumers' needs if they hope to design products, services, and processes that will please and retain customers. Complicating the situation even further, companies are coming under increasing pressure to demonstrate reliable profits—even as consumer behavior and attitudes become ever more difficult to discern.

But the situation isn't impossible. As the articles in this volume make clear, managers at the most customer-savvy companies are developing new, more effective ways to clarify consumers' needs, including observing people as they're using products and services, analyzing customers' stories about their purchases, and using the Web to gather information about specific customer groups. Many organizations are also getting better at identifying customer segments based on customers' profitability, willingness to spread positive word of mouth, and other key defining characteristics. Armed with new insights into who customers are and what they want, managers are designing better approaches to communicating with consumers and further strengthening their loyalty.

No business can survive for very long without getting to know its customers. As a manager, you can support this effort in numerous ways—no matter where you work in your organization. The articles in this book can help. Here's a quick preview of the tools, techniques, and tactics you'll find in the following pages.

Understanding Customers' Needs

Getting to know your customers starts with discerning their needs—the benefits they hope to gain by selecting a particular product or service, and the results they expect your company's offerings to deliver. The articles in this section reveal powerful new techniques companies are using to answer that most crucial of questions: What *do* customers want?

Business writer Kristen Donahue opens the section with her article "Tuning In to Your Customers," in which she assesses numerous experts' recommendations for understanding customers' needs. Want to grasp what's most important to your company's customers? Consider using a trendspotting consultancy to identify what consumers will care about most in the soon-to-arrive future. Watch consumers using your and other companies' products in a natural setting to gauge how they feel about the offering, what difficulties they encounter in using it, and what will motivate them to buy it. And invite your online customers to share their ideas about how to improve your company's offerings.

In "Let the Customer Make the Case," consultant Gerald Berstell and DePaul University professor Denise Nitterhouse explain how to collect and analyze stories about consumers' purchases to gain insights into the roles people want products to perform for them. Using what these authors call the customer case research method, you can track the events, thoughts, and experiences that have led people to spend money on products that help them grapple with real-life tasks.

Gathering customer case research entails giving in-depth interviews, observing customer behavior, and reviewing customer documents—including shopping lists, vendor files, and catalogs perused. By analyzing these materials, you identify new opportunities for your company to appeal to consumers. For instance, one automobile tire manufacturer discovered that many people bought replacement tires not in response to a flat but to reduce road noise so they could better enjoy the high-end car stereo system they had just installed. Result? The company saw an opportunity to develop low-noise tires to satisfy this unexpected need.

In "How Best Buy's Executives Learn from the Front Lines," business writer Lauren Keller Johnson explains how a retailing behemoth uses another valuable source of information to identify customer needs. At Best Buy, corporate officers realized that frontline employees and their managers are ideally positioned to generate creative ideas for serving customers. To take advantage of this positioning, the company has developed a "reverse mentoring" program to support its renowned Customer Centricity initiative.

Through this program, officers spend time in Best Buy stores, observing general managers and employees in action and developing ideas for better supporting stores' efforts to serve customers. For example, one officer who spent time in a high-performing store decided that more flexible scheduling to accommodate stores' diverse talent pools would enable Best Buy to tap its workforce's expertise better and thus provide higher-quality service to store visitors. By making more shifts available for employees with different scheduling needs, the company would better retain the talented, knowledgeable workers it needed to satisfy customers.

This section ends with business writer Jim Billington's article "The Fourfold Path to Figuring Out What Your Customers Really Want." Billington provides additional useful tips for understanding customers' needs, including considering the context in which target customers shop for certain products. For instance, one food company found that when men shop for cookies for a poker game, they often go to a convenience store and purchase several high-priced brands. But when they're doing the weekly shopping for their spouses, many men like to bargain shop by purchasing large quantities of cookies and they like to complete the errand as quickly as possible. To serve the different needs that arise in these two shopping contexts, the food company could develop two strategies: place pricey, smaller-sized cookie packages in convenience stores, and position bulk cookies in grocery stores close to aisle fronts—in full, easy view of fast-moving male shoppers. "It's the same customer you're trying to attract," notes Billington, "but in two very different contexts."

Identifying Customer Segments

By understanding your customers' diverse needs, you can identify customer segments—groups of consumers with unique needs you can satisfy through specific products, services, and processes. The articles in this section explain how to define customer segments based on particular criteria and how to use technology to further segment your customers.

The section opens with "Tuning In to the Voice of Your Customer," by Bain & Company global strategy expert James Allen, Bain director emeritus Frederick Reichheld, and Bain partner Barney Hamilton. These authors recommend segmenting customers based on their profitability (the revenues they bring in minus the costs of serving them), as well as their tendency to act as advocates for your company by singing the organization's praises to friends. The ultimate goal? To shift ever more customers into the high-profit, high-advocacy area by designing and delivering offers and experiences tailored to their preferences.

In "What's the Cure for Customer Fatigue?" Harvard Business School Press executive editor Kirsten Sandberg explains how to segment customers based on their potential to drive business growth *across* product and service lines. For instance, a financial services company might segment its customer base into these categories: "boomers who are downscaling, shifting to lower-paying but more emotionally rewarding jobs; boomers who are financially responsible for the care of their aging parents; parents saving for their children's education; and single women looking to buy a home."

To serve these segments, the financial services company could assign one group of service reps to each segment and train those reps to sell the company's entire line of offerings to that segment—instead of having reps for each offering contact each customer separately. Through this approach, the company acquires "a richer view of the customer's needs and desires, [and] a subtler understanding of how its brands fit into the customer's lifestyle and changing life circumstances compared to competing brands."

Business writer Jean Ayers shares marketing experts' additional insights into customer segmentation in "Do

You Really Know What to Do with Your Customer Data?" For instance, Harvard Business School professor Gerald Zaltman uses one-on-one interviews and other techniques to understand the beliefs, emotions, and unconscious attitudes that different groups of consumers have regarding a product or brand. By understanding the unique bundles of associations that diverse consumer groups have for a product, companies can reinforce those associations through targeted marketing campaigns and specific offerings. To illustrate, General Motors found that some customers associated buying GM vehicles with patriotism: by purchasing from GM, "they saw themselves as not simply helping Americans keep their jobs, but as fulfilling a larger obligation that they felt toward their country." Informed by this insight, the company could develop communications that appealed specifically to this customer segment's emotions.

The final article in this section, "Survey Your Customers—Electronically," explains how to use the Web to gather information about specific customer segments. For example, a drug company "found the Web valuable in tracking down people with obscure ailments for which the [firm] is developing treatments." The article also identifies the challenges of this approach—including the growing need to provide incentives for people to answer questions online, and the bias that can arise when certain groups (such as older people and rural residents) are underrepresented in online survey responses.

Communicating with Customers

Once you better understand your customers' needs and you've segmented customers based on their unique requirements, you can communicate more effectively with them through a variety of means. The articles in this section present helpful techniques.

For example, in "Zeroing In on What Customers Really Want," business writer Douglas Smith explains how to adapt your customer communications to satisfy three innate psychological needs. These needs are *competence* (enhancements in knowledge or ability), *autonomy* (the power to make choices without pressure from a company), and *relatedness* (the sense that a company genuinely cares about its customers). Smith offers ideas for serving each of these needs while communicating with customers. Though his suggestions apply to formal sales presentations, you can put the same principles into practice during other types of communications. To promote competence, for instance, present the main points of your communication quickly as highlights. To ensure autonomy, talk with your customer as you would to a neighbor. And to create relatedness, acknowledge customers' needs and use their language.

In "Are You Reaching Your Customers?" business writer Richard Bierck explains how to craft more effective messages for customers—not only through your company's formal communication vehicles but also through its choice of product or service offerings. According to Bierck, "many [companies'] communication errors stem from a naïve belief among [managers] that they're necessarily trying to connect with people exactly like themselves. For example, [they] overlook issues of nationality, language, ethnicity, and age." As an illustration, Bierck cites a restaurant chain in south Florida that lacks menus printed in Spanish—even though the area is heavily populated by Hispanics. He offers another example of a drugstore chain in Washington, D.C., that sells hundreds of products for blondes, despite the fact that it serves primarily an African American clientele.

The article "Connecting with Your Customers" provides additional guidelines for effective communications—including ways to determine when to foster a long-term relationship with a customer and when to cross-sell your company's products or services. This article also presents strategies for creating a feeling of interpersonal connection while communicating with a customer. As it turns out, something as seemingly simple as a smile can strongly influence a customer's response to your message. For instance, in one study, cocktail-lounge customers who were approached by a server wearing a broad smile left more than twice as much in tips, on average, than customers who were greeted with minimal smiles.

Harvard Business School assistant professor Frances Frei concludes this section on communication with her article "Beyond the Carrot and the Stick: New Alternatives for Influencing Customer Behavior." According to Frei, you can influence your company's customers to behave in ways that benefit the organization by evoking social norms and peer pressure. For example, employees at JetBlue reduced cabin cleaning time and accelerated airplane turnover at gates by asking each customer to clean up his or her area before leaving the aircraft. The employees pointed out to travelers that by pitching in, they could help keep fares low. "Customers responded positively," Frei notes. "Even those who might not have been eager to help didn't want to stick out as shirkers."

Enhancing Customer Loyalty

One key benefit of getting to know your company's customers is the enhanced loyalty such understanding can foster. The articles in this section take a closer look at loyalty—including why it's important, how to measure it, and how to enhance it.

Consultant Uta Werner opens the section with her article "Do You Know How Much Your Customers Are Really Worth to You?" In it, Werner presents a three-step process for calculating a loyal customer's lifetime value. First, identify the customer's initial "main" purchase and the related products and services acquired over time. Second, figure the profitability of these purchases, taking into account net pricing, charges for capital used, and so forth. Third, create a timeline showing the profit stream over the customer's lifetime, discounting the stream at the cost of capital. If the resulting number is positive, the customer is generating value for your company.

Of course, creating loyal customers hinges on turning first-time buyers into repeat purchasers. Corporate adviser Jill Griffin offers tips for fostering this transformation in "Five Questions About Customer Loyalty with Jill Griffin." According to Griffin, companies are particularly vulnerable to customer defection after acquiring a new customer. Why? First-time buyers are triers: they're looking for confirmation that their purchase decision was wise. If they experience any problems in post-purchase service (a missing product part, service delivered too late), they'll regret their choice and won't likely do business with your company again.

Griffin offers ideas for cultivating customer loyalty after that initial sale. For example, coordinate all touch points (order fulfillment, billing, returns, postsale service) to deliver a seamless experience to customers. Use frequent follow-up contact to assess customer satisfaction. But to avoid annoying customers, add value with every contact. To illustrate, an automobile salesperson sends a new customer a follow-up thank-you note—and encloses an article about road safety with a note saying, "Thought you might find this interesting."

In "Five Keys to Keeping Your Best Customers," Jim Billington provides additional suggestions for strengthening customer loyalty—including analyzing the reasons behind defections. For example, create "failure analysis teams, each headed by a senior manager, each member charged with interviewing 10 to 25 defectors." Use the classic "five why's" to identify the root causes of defection: Question: "Why did you stop using our product?" Answer: "I got a better deal from your competitor." Question: "Why was his a better deal?" And so on. Often, Billington notes, customers initially cite price as the reason for their defection. But by asking them the five why's, you'll likely discover that other complaints (such as poor service) were more important. Armed with this knowledge, you can develop ways to address those complaints—and keep customers from jumping ship.

The next article in this section, "A Crash Course in Customer Relationship Management," presents a primer on CRM, an approach that enables companies to identify and differentiate their key customers, interact with them in mutually beneficial ways, and customize their offerings to customer segments. The article explains the benefits of CRM and describes technologies (such as customer databases, Web sites, and computerized customization of products) that help companies cultivate connections with millions of consumers. According to this selection, your firm can best benefit from CRM if its customers have highly differentiated needs and value to the organization.

Business writer David Stauffer concludes this section with additional loyalty-enhancing strategies in his article "What Customer-Centric Really Means: Seven Key Insights." For example, Stauffer maintains that everyone in an organization—not just frontline workers—must learn to see things from the customer's perspective rather than the company's perspective. This external focus can increase customers' perceptions of product and service quality and further deepen their loyalty. For instance, suppose a parking-lot attendant at a medical center helps a patient who uses a wheelchair determine how to get to the hospital two blocks away. In this case, the patient will likely feel more loyal to the hospital—even though the lot attendant would hardly strike most people as a frontline employee in the healthcare industry.

Clearly, getting to know your company's customers requires significant effort. But the payoff is well worth it—no matter where in your organization you work. As you read the selections in this volume, start applying your new knowledge by considering the following questions:

- What steps might you take to deepen your understanding of customers' needs? For instance, could you launch a field research project in which you observe consumers' use of particular products or services? If you work in a department or unit that doesn't typically initiate such projects, are there other managers in the company who might be conducting such efforts? If so, how might you gain access to their results? And what do the results suggest about how your own group might help the company better serve its customers?

- By what criteria does your company segment its customers? If you don't know, whom in the organization might you contact to find out? What are managers throughout your firm doing to serve the unique needs that characterize each customer segment? How might you and your team better serve those needs?

- Under what circumstances do you typically communicate with your company's customers? Consider communications channels beyond just face-to-face or phone or e-mail exchanges with customers. For example, a product user's manual that your team has developed, an invoice that your group sends, and an in-store merchandise display that your department has designed all constitute communication channels that send messages to your firm's customers. To what extent do your communications with customers acknowledge and address their needs? How might you make these communications more effective?

- How loyal are your company's customers? What steps might you and your team take to enhance customer loyalty? Consider strategies such as coordinating touch points to create a seamless experience for customers, discovering and addressing reasons for defections, and leveraging CRM technology.

Understanding Customers' Needs

• • •

Getting to know your customers starts with discerning their needs—the benefits they hope to gain by selecting a particular product or service, and the results they expect your company's offerings to deliver. The articles in this section reveal powerful new techniques companies are using to answer that most crucial of questions: What *do* customers want?

In the pages that follow, you'll find suggestions for gathering insights about customer preferences—including observing consumers as they use products or services, analyzing their stories about why they decided to purchase a particular offering, and asking frontline managers and employees for ideas.

Tuning In to
Your Customers

• • •

Kristen B. Donahue

Today's customers are marketing enigmas. It's hard to pin down what they need and what they'll buy—and how to make them want to buy it from you. Vast sources of free information means the balance of power has shifted to the consumer—you can no longer get in the door with traditional smoke-and-mirrors marketing.

At the same time, profit is back in fashion as a *raison d'être*: now more than ever, managers are expected to deliver strong products and services with on-target, effective marketing programs.

So how do you make sure you're not wasting your valuable product development and marketing budgets? Do whatever you can to get your finger on the pulse of the markets you are trying to reach. This requires being able to identify trends in society as a whole and in your target audience in particular, and being able to adapt to changing sociocultural needs. Fortunately, you don't need to possess psychic powers to divine this knowledge. Here, we examine how to get a sense of what is important to your customers and how to get them to listen—and react—to you.

Predicting the Future: Trendspotting

Imagine a crystal ball that reveals the shape of things to come and, more specifically, what consumers will care about. Armed with this information, companies could design products and services to appeal perfectly to their customers' needs. An entire field of consultancies has sprung up claiming to be that crystal ball—identifying a number of general trends and charging hefty fees to tell leading corporations whether their product ideas are "on trend" or not. A well-known trendspotter is Faith Popcorn, whose best-selling book, *The Popcorn Report*, describes 16 trends that are affecting the world. Among them: *Cocooning* ("the need to protect oneself from the harsh, unpredictable realities of the outside world"); *Vigilante Consumer* ("Frustrated, often angry consumers are manipulating the marketplace through pressure, protest and politics"); and *Fantasy Adventure* ("the modern age whets our desire for roads untaken"). Popcorn's most recent book, *EVEolution*, adds one more trend to the list: "The way women think and behave . . . is impacting business, causing a marketing shift away from a hierarchical model toward a relational one." (Popcorn herself sets an example by using that trend to cash in on the needs of women: The Faith Popcorn Home Office Cocoon Collection, advertised on her consulting firm's Web site, is a suite of furniture designed specifically for women—complete with a raised desktop to accommodate women who work with their legs crossed and an attached bud vase on the credenza.) Iconoculture, a trendcasting firm, has come up with its own set of 40 cultural trends that are described in its book, *The Future Ain't What It Used to Be*. Along with the trend descriptions, Iconoculture identifies a number of opportunities predicted to arise from the trends and urges readers to stake out these territories with their careers, businesses, and brands.

While the trends identified by Popcorn, Iconoculture, and others may seem like nothing more than creative interpretations of good old common sense, the interpretations they offer can provide a useful framework for how your products and services will fit into your customers' lives—use them as guidelines to influence what kinds of products you develop and how you market them to your customers.

Become Your Customer

No, it's not a lesson in Zen mastery. It's about going into the trenches and witnessing firsthand the needs of your

Are Focus Groups Useful?

The origins of focus groups date back to World War II, when a group of sociologists showed military propaganda films to small groups of citizens and asked them questions about their reactions and perceptions. The marketing uses of in-depth group interviewing soon became obvious—and the method of asking small groups of consumers about their needs and opinions became a staple in the market research toolbox.

Rather than providing quantifiable responses to specific questions, "focus group participants provide a flow of input and interaction related to the topic or group of topics that the group is centered around," writes Holly Edmunds in *The Focus Group Research Handbook*. The result is an understanding of the target audience's perspectives, feelings, and motivations that can't be obtained through quantitative studies such as telephone interviews and mail surveys.

Focus groups are most useful when you want to evaluate a new concept or idea and "the best evaluation comes from letting the target customer . . . view the concept directly," writes Edmunds. An example is an ad agency that wants to test a new campaign to see if the message is clear to consumers and whether it would prompt them to purchase the product. The agency can get a sense of these things by showing the ad to consumers and observing their reactions and their likes and dislikes.

Another common use of focus groups is testing product concepts. Participants offer their reactions to detailed descriptions of products or even prototypes, and product developers can use their observations to tweak the product design—or, if it's negatively received, go back to the drawing board.

There are hazards to using focus groups, however. They are qualitative studies, which means that the results cannot be tied to percentages or statistics. Focus group results reflect only a very small segment of the market and cannot be applied to the population as a whole. Therefore, there are many situations where focus groups really can't add value. For example, they should not be used to set prices for a product or service, or to make a final decision.

The answer? Use focus groups wisely. Before you sign off on a request for focus group funding, make sure your expectations are in line. "Consider focus groups only to be a 'thermometer' that allows you to test the 'temperature' of consumers' reactions to your research topic," cautions Edmunds. "It should be considered only as one aspect of the decision-making process, rather than as the process itself."

Source: *The Focus Group Research Handbook*, by Holly Edmunds, 1999, American Marketing Association.

customers—how they use your products or your competitors'. How do they feel? What do they want from the product? What will motivate them to buy it? You can start to chip away at the answers to these questions in a formal focus group setting, but nothing gets to the core of consumer motivation like watching them interact with the products in a natural setting.

A recent *Fast Company* article describes how Burton Snowboards, a well-known snowboard company, keeps constant contact with a core group of users to determine how their needs are being met by the Burton products. The users in question are a group of 300 professional riders, some of whom are on Burton's pro team, writes Rekha Balu. "Almost every day, staffers talk to those riders—on the slopes and on the phone. If one of them has a suggestion or a problem, a Burton employee calls back within 24 hours, sometimes attending to one of those 300 riders before helping retailers or other customers." To make sure that the desires of the pro riders are in line with the needs of amateur customers, Balu continues, Burton sends its reps out on the slopes each weekend to offer demo equipment and watch how riders use it: "Instead of toting clipboards and 50-question surveys, the reps listen to riders and watch what works and what doesn't." In the past five years, Balu reports, Burton's market share has gone from 30% to 40%.

Seek Real Input from Your Online Customers

Customer input on the Internet can extend far beyond a "feedback" button on your home page, writes permission marketing expert Nick Usborne in an online article. To build lasting relationships with your customers, he suggests implementing a Visitor Advisory Board (VAB).

It's an opportunity to "invite your visitors and customers to take a real part in the development and improvement of your online business." Usborne suggests devoting an area on your company's home page to soliciting VAB

> A successful word-of-mouth campaign depends not just on *how many* people get the message but on *who* is spreading—and receiving—it.

members. Provide a way for them to tell you what products, improvements, or information they'd like to see and how the Web site could be more useful to them. Offer an incentive such as an opportunity to speak to the CEO when one of their ideas is implemented or a password-accessible area with links to discounted products.

It's all about the relationship, Usborne writes. "You'll get invaluable input on usability, customer experience, and merchandising issues," as well as "a core group of customers who will support you as you grow—because they'll know and feel that they played a part in that growth." Even more, VAB members will likely become your strongest advocates: "Once you have this group of enthusiasts helping you out," Usborne writes, "you can be sure that they'll help spread the word. After all, if they've been part of the process, they'll want others to see what they've been involved with."

Get the Right People to Spread Your Message

"Word of mouth is—even in this age of mass communications and multimillion dollar advertising campaigns—still the most important form of human communication," writes Malcolm Gladwell in *The Tipping Point: How Little Things Can Make a Big Difference*. Gladwell says that a successful word-of-mouth campaign depends not just on *how many* people get the message but on *who* is spreading—and receiving—it. He describes the three kinds of people who are essential to social epidemics: Connectors, Mavens, and Salesmen.

Connectors are "people with an extraordinary knack of making friends and acquaintances." An example is Paul Revere, whose famous "midnight ride" from Boston to the town of Lexington alerted enough people of the British plan to attack that the Americans were able to soundly beat them in what became the beginning of the American Revolution. It wasn't just that Revere was out knocking on doors—another man, William Dawes, made a similar ride that same night, covering a similar amount of distance, but he failed to incite the same reaction as

Revere did. What made the difference was the kind of people Revere knew and talked to—influential community leaders—and the respect he himself had in the community.

Mavens are people who have an extraordinary interest in and knowledge of market activities who also like to share that information with others. Mavens have the knowledge and the social skills to start word-of-mouth epidemics, Gladwell writes. What sets them apart, though, is "not so much what they know but how they pass it along. The fact that Mavens want to help, for no other reason than because they like to help, turns out to be an awfully effective way of getting someone's attention." Gladwell cites as an example the popularity of the Zagat restaurant guides, which consist of reviews written by consumers. "Their real power derives from the fact that the reviews are the reports of volunteers—of diners who want to share their opinions with others. Somehow that represents a more compelling recommendation than the opinion of an expert whose job it is to rate restaurants."

Mavens are information brokers, writes Gladwell. Their role is to share what they know—they do not persuade. However, for a social epidemic to occur, people must be convinced to do something. Enter the third group of people: Salesmen. Their role is to persuade people when they are unconvinced of what they are hearing. These salesmen rely on their obvious charisma as well as subtle, hidden, and unspoken messages, and they do the job of convincing people that what they've been hearing about is relevant to them.

Getting the market's attention will continue to be a challenge—that's a trend we feel safe predicting. Stay alert to what your customers say and do and watch for cultural trends that you can cash in on. Knowing how to catch a glimpse into the collective psyche of your customers can only help.

For Further Reading

The Future Ain't What It Used to Be by Iconoculture, Inc. (Mary Meehan, Larry Samuel, and Vickie Abrahamson) (1998, Riverhead Books)

EVEolution by Faith Popcorn (2000, Hyperion)

"Listen Up!" by Rekha Balu (*Fast Company,* Issue 34, May 2000)

The Popcorn Report by Faith Popcorn (1992, Harperbusiness)

The Tipping Point: How Little Things Can Make a Difference by Malcolm Gladwell (2000, Little, Brown)

Reprint C0104D

Let the Customer Make the Case

• • •

Gerald Berstell and Denise Nitterhouse

The jobs-to-be-done theory holds that products are successful when they connect with a circumstance—with a job that customers find themselves needing to be done . . .

By identifying what jobs people really care about and developing products that make it easier to achieve these jobs, companies can identify new markets that they were previously unaware of and that could not be uncovered via traditional market research.

—Seeing What's Next: Using the Theories of Innovation
to Predict Industry Change

If, as the text above makes clear, "traditional market research" can't discern what sorts of jobs potential customers are looking to do, what type of research can?

Our studies have shown that collecting and analyzing the stories behind purchases can provide deep and invaluable insights into jobs-to-be-done, much more so than traditional surveys or focus groups. To get at the real reasons behind a customer purchase, we use a process we call customer case research (CCR). It's a method that tracks the events, thoughts, and experiences that lead people to spend money on products that will help them deal with real-life circumstances.

Customer case researchers are not survey takers collecting attribute data, nor are they moderators seeking opinions and attitudes or ethnographers observing how people use products. Instead, they work like investigative reporters or detectives, tracking down the whole story behind a specific event—in this instance, a single purchase.

Much CCR has been conducted for organizations seeking to boost the performance of existing products. The results can give managers and companies a vivid understanding of what jobs people are really looking to get done and the circumstances that generate those jobs. The dramatic pictures of customer situations CCR produces can generate ideas not only for retooling existing products or businesses but also for initiating new ones. Even if the latter is not among the original research goals, it's a frequent byproduct of all CCR projects.

Conducting Customer Case Research

Customer case researchers interview customers to chart the trail of circumstances, events, people, experiences, actions, and thoughts that led them to buy a product or service. Studies begin with the question "Can you tell me about the circumstances that started you on the path to making this purchase at this time?" Researchers encourage participants to tell their stories in their own words. Nobody is forced to select from preset multiple-choice responses.

Interviews are structured according to the chronology of the customer's story—the circumstances that start the story, and the events, experiences, and thought processes that lead to its conclusion. Unlike most market research that focuses on product, CCR concentrates on the customers and their experiences. It doesn't prioritize topics but, rather, lets the stories determine what's most significant.

> The richest interactions between customer and product often take place during the purchase process.

Researchers build their cases through a combination of in-depth interviews, observation, and reviews of customer documents such as shopping lists, vendor files, or catalogues used. As they pursue the complete stories behind purchases, researchers often uncover unexpected situations in many parts of the process. They explore the dynamics of actual buying decisions made in the context of real supply constraints, timing pressures, and even career tensions. Researchers pursue a story until they feel they fully understand the path that led to the purchase-decision outcome.

> Are people using the product in ways you didn't expect? This signals a gap in the market.

CCR is so productive because the richest interactions between customer and product often take place during the purchase process. People seeking a product are generally more aware of their circumstances and jobs-to-be-done than they are when later using that product. Indeed, for a wide range of products such as home mortgages, life insurance, and gifts, the only time most people are actively involved with the product is during the purchase process.

Case researchers continue their work until they stop uncovering new jobs and underlying circumstances. Consumer product case research generally produces a comfortably exhaustive list of jobs-to-be-done by investigating

Targeting Participants

Participants are chosen for CCR based on their potential to provide a rich variety of circumstances and jobs-to-be-done. The most rewarding stories often are provided by:

- Switchers: Customers who frequently change vendors, even without price incentives. These customers may have jobs that aren't being done to their satisfaction. They're often more likely to point the way to tomorrow's products than are customers content with current offerings.
- Polygamists: Customers who use multiple vendors for the same product. Marketers usually try to place each customer into one demographic slot with one buying process, but in fact, a single customer may buy the same product in different ways to fit several different jobs.
- Newbies: New customers, or those who have recently increased purchases significantly. Case research on buyers making these shifts can uncover new jobs that can spur increased opportunity.

In business-to-business CCR, salespeople and databases can directly identify customers with these characteristics. CCR for consumer durables can identify participants through customer registrations. Retailers can intercept store traffic. Packaged-goods makers usually have to look for participants in places where the product is purchased or used.

100 or fewer cases. Business-to-business research generally involves case studies of 25 customers making approximately 100 purchases for different sites, applications, and departments. Some very productive CCR projects have been built on fewer than 10 case studies. Quantitative research methods can be used to measure the prevalence of the circumstances and jobs-to-be-done that CCR discovers.

While observational research can show how people use a wide range of products, it may never reveal the circumstances that compel their need in the first place.

Analyzing Cases

When reviewing cases, look for the following indicators of new jobs-to-be-done opportunities:

Surprising Start Points

Purchase stories always begin with the circumstances that trigger the purchase process. Are customers starting off in places you didn't expect? A project collecting more than 100 case studies of replacement-tire purchases found very few actually resulted from a flat tire. More began with the customer recently buying a high-end car stereo system or car cell phone that suddenly made them aware of tire-generated road noise that impaired the audibility of the new devices. The tire makers who commissioned the research had not yet discovered the job-to-be-done of improving a car's acoustical environment for new audio devices.

Unexpected Product Uses

Are people using the product in ways you didn't expect? When this happens, it signals a gap in the market that's just waiting to be filled. This creates opportunities to reposition an existing product to fit the job people have unexpectedly used the product for or to develop a new product that accomplishes the job better than the solutions customers have already stumbled upon.

For instance, while today we take for granted the availability of microwave ovens in the office, as well as the plethora of microwaveable meals available, in the 1980s, consumer product companies were slow to see the opportunity created for them by newly proliferating office microwaves. One way they discovered this niche was through CCR into a new product originally marketed as a fresh, gourmet, at-home dinner alternative to frozen TV dinners. CCR found that early buyers of these refrigerated dinner entrées were instead taking them to their offices to use as lunches that were quicker, healthier, and priced more economically than traditional office lunch options.

These first purchasers were extremely articulate about

the difficulties they had filling the job-to-be-done of getting lunch at work and the way in which they saw office microwaves enabling new options.

Unforeseen Obstacles to Purchase

Are people having purchasing problems that you didn't anticipate? Where do their stories hit snags? Tracking the purchase processes often uncovers difficult tradeoffs that people are forced to make between products that weren't designed with their job-to-be-done in mind. Researchers can uncover not only the circumstances that kick off the purchase process but also the events that arise as people pursue it. Some of these circumstances put the spotlight on opportunities to reduce obstacles through innovative distribution, pricing, and promotional strategies.

For example, an innovative multimedia corporate training system attracted only six customers during its first nine months on the market. The system required a $40,000, one-year lease of courseware along with the purchase of $3,000 worth of hardware on which to run the courses. When potential corporate customers balked, saying they didn't have the money for this, CCR discovered that, surprisingly, it wasn't the $40,000 lease that posed a problem; it was the need to justify the $3,000 hardware purchase that intimidated customers. This insight led to a reworking of the company's business model. The new strategy called for hardware to be given away for "free" while lease prices were raised to accommodate the change. The reworked pricing propelled the company's product to a successful launch, and the company's stock price multiplied eightfold within the next three years.

Unexpected People

Do purchase case studies reveal unanticipated customer demographics? It's extremely common for business-to-business case studies to uncover people that nobody knew

---

Using CCR to Support Emerging Strategies

Perhaps CCR's most powerful role in supporting innovation is in its ability to help companies settle on the appropriate strategy for a new product. Conduct research on the first purchases of a new product, right after it's introduced to the market. Whether the product is yours or a competitor's, you want to hear from real customers who have bought the product. It will give you insight into the unexpected circumstances, jobs, people, obstacles, and segmentation dimensions that will let you drive the way the market evolves.

Extremely valuable jobs-to-be-done insights also can be drawn from companies that have consented to be beta test sites for new products. The decision to become a beta test site is fraught with many of the same perils as an actual purchase.

---

were involved in purchasing decisions and acquisitions. These people may have jobs-to-be-done that differ from that of the targeted purchaser. Discovering these heretofore unknown purchasers may not prompt a product redesign but may instead suggest promotion and communication innovations that benefit these newly discovered purchasers whether they come from business-to-business or consumer arenas.

Consumer CCR into women's jewelry found a substantial submarket of male purchasers needing to complete a job that no jewelry retailer had anticipated. It turned out that purchasing the piece of jewelry fulfilled only half the job many men needed to get done. In addition to the fine gift, these men also needed romantic and surprising ways to present it. CCR helped one retailer learn that a key to success in this market was collecting and sharing ways to do this.

New Segmentation Dimensions

When an individual buyer relates different purchase stories for the same product, it's a clear sign he's facing multiple jobs-to-be-done, and it's highly likely that at least one of those jobs isn't being well filled.

This situation was best illustrated by a situation described in *The Innovator's Solution: Creating and Sustaining Successful Growth*, by Clayton M. Christensen and Michael E. Raynor. The authors explained what happened when a quick-service restaurant chain used CCR to figure out how to improve profits on its line of milkshakes. The chain discovered that rather than buying milkshakes to slake thirst or enhance a given meal, customer segmentation actually broke down into two surprisingly diverse groups: individuals who purchased the drinks in the morning and parents of young children who bought the drinks in the evening. The morning purchasers were buying milkshakes to have something to "do" during a long and boring commute, while the evening purchasers were using the drink to placate their children after spending the day denying them other less reasonable requests. This unexpected information gave the chain the option of creating new products geared to the specific needs of these two surprising niche groups.

After collecting case studies from one or two dozen people, look at the different outcomes and itemize the factors that pushed purchasers in different directions. Though sometimes these will be demographic, most often you'll find that the keys are different circumstances and jobs-to-be-done.

When to Conduct CCR

By definition, case studies can be conducted only around real purchases of real products. To evaluate new product ideas, conduct case studies of current products believed to address the same customer circumstances. Although customer case research starts with an existing product, remember that the focus is not on the product—existing or new—but on the circumstances and jobs-to-be-done that drive people to buy it. If a competitor is already making a similar product, use CCR into purchases of that product to acquire insights into circumstances and jobs; these insights will help your new product leapfrog over the original entrant.

Customer case studies can also get cross-functional new product teams—including individuals involved in R&D, marketing, sales operations, and service—into the circumstances of the customer and inspire vigorous discussions of how to respond to the jobs-to-be-done they create. And the circumstances that trigger and shape purchase actions often translate directly into 4-P (product, promotion, pricing, and placement) strategies.

Understanding the real reasons why customers buy existing products can not only help spur the creation of new products to better answer a customer's real need, but it can also help marketers understand the circumstances driving a specific purchase. This will make them better equipped to craft messages that speak directly to those circumstances, then place those messages in the most appropriate venues. Exploring purchase circumstances also reveals the costs people actually incur when trying to complete those purchases and can point the way to pricing opportunities and strategies. Unearthing purchase circumstances often also presents unexpected opportunities to use previously unconsidered distribution channels that are more easily accessed by targeted purchasers.

Reprint S0503C

How Best Buy's Executives Learn from the Front Lines

• • •

Lauren Keller Johnson

How well do you leverage your frontline employees' expertise? If your company is like most, the answer is "not very well."

And what a waste that is. Your frontline workers have a unique vantage point on your business. They are on the phone or interacting face-to-face with customers every day, and they have firsthand familiarity with your products and services.

Compared with corporate officers, frontline employees and their managers are ideally positioned to generate creative ideas for serving customers and eliciting top-notch performances from themselves and their teams.

So why have so few companies systematized a "bottom-up" process of extracting fresh thinking from the field and feeding promising ideas back to their senior executive teams? Some organizations get sidetracked by other seemingly more pressing initiatives. Others are too busy grappling with rapid changes in the business landscape to establish the systems required to leverage their workforce's expertise.

Yet a handful of enterprises have overcome such obstacles—and scored remarkable successes. Best Buy, a retailer of technology and entertainment products and services, is one of them.

At the heart of Best Buy's efforts is a unique program that connects corporate officers with in-the-field operations in retail outlets.

Engaging Employees, Focusing on Customers

In 2003, Best Buy introduced a now well-publicized initiative called "Customer Centricity," meant to give new focus to the needs of Best Buy's diverse customer mix. In an early 2004 press release, CEO Brad Anderson described the program's merits: the "initiative enables us to engage more deeply with customers by empowering our employees to deliver tailored products, solutions, and services to customers . . . This work has allowed us to look at our business through a new lens."

Here was the problem: the lens Anderson was looking through may have been new, but it still came from headquarters, not from the front lines. And therein lay a dilemma: Can you really connect with your customers in Boston, Houston, and Atlanta from your office in the suburbs of Minneapolis?

Corporate officers soon realized the answer was no. "Officers weren't in touch with the field," says Tim McGeehan, executive vice president of retail sales.

To address this disconnect, the company reached out to store managers. "We brought six general managers [store managers] in from across the country and asked them what an appropriate program for addressing this situation might look like," says Steve Prather, an internal communications executive at Best Buy. The general managers (GMs) suggested a radical notion, reversing the traditional mentoring model: store managers would serve as mentors to the corporate officers.

In September 2004, the company piloted the new GM mentoring program, pairing Best Buy's top 130 officers with the top-performing 130 stores. The first stage of the program called for each executive to spend three days working in an assigned store during the fall. The visits would clarify for the executive what enabled a high-performing store's success and broaden his thinking on what the corporate support center could do to further drive that success. For example, one logistics officer focused his visit on helping stores ensure on-time deliveries and get freight to the sales floor faster. Meanwhile, a retail officer sought ways to improve shoppers' in-store experiences.

But as these executives were bringing to bear their expertise to improve store operations, they were also being mentored in the realities of the business by managers and workers on Best Buy's front lines.

During the second stage, store managers would spend a week during the winter and spring of 2005 visiting the corporate center: sitting in on meetings and phone calls, and providing ideas for improving executive support of the stores.

From Field to Corporate Office

McGeehan was a developer of and participant in the pilot. "I've been in the retail field a long time," he says, "but you see things through a different lens when you spend a few days with a store manager on his turf." McGeehan maintains he saw a powerful "human element" at play during his visit to Nashua, N.H.

For example, he noticed that his mentor, Janet Farley, then a general manager, "cut people some slack" based on her knowledge of their personal challenges. A single parent who came in late for a shift, for example, wouldn't have to fear for her job. McGeehan took this observation back to the corporate office and suggested more flexible scheduling to accommodate stores' diverse talent pools. "By making more shifts available for employees with different needs, we could tap their expertise better," he explains.

Jennifer Driscoll, vice president of investor relations, visited a Houston-area store in January 2005, where she was mentored by GM Brett Byrum. Asking Byrum to describe his most pressing challenges, Driscoll learned that his store was struggling with ineffective phone systems and inventory-ordering processes. Upon her return to headquarters, she shared his comments with other officers and discovered that their mentors had cited the same problems. The executive team took action by seeing that technologies were installed that enabled store

> ## "It was a powerful experience to see a corporate officer show interest in my teams."

managers to order inventory directly from the floor and by having the phone systems upgraded.

How did store managers' experience compare with that of corporate officers? Byrum offers his impressions. Recruited by Best Buy from Wal-Mart in 2004, Byrum was excited by the concept of the program. "But I was also hesitant," he says. "I wasn't sure what my role would be, or how I could demonstrate value for the officers."

Yet, he says, "It was a powerful experience to see a corporate officer show interest in my teams—even the part-time employees."

During the visit, Driscoll shadowed Byrum and let him and his employees know she was there to help. "She asked questions more than giving advice," Byrum says. "By the time she left, everyone in the store felt they now knew someone at the corporate center who they could talk to on the phone directly."

During his April 2005 visit to the corporate center, Byrum met with Driscoll and other officers, answering questions about his store's challenges and sitting in on earnings meetings and phone conferences with analysts. When analysts asked questions about Best Buy store operations that Driscoll couldn't answer—for instance, how the company's return policy worked and which accessories were sold with hit products such as PlayStation Portable—Byrum provided the requested information. Moreover, according to Driscoll, Byrum offered helpful feedback on how the officers could define customer centricity to investors.

Reaping Benefits

Though still in its infancy, Best Buy's GM mentoring initiative has already changed the dynamics of Best Buy's communications structure.

"With most retailers, there's a 12-lane communication highway going from corporate out to the stores and a dirt road from the stores to corporate," says McGeehan. "We've now got a highway going both ways—with many more access points between GMs and officers." He also believes the program has "flipped the company upside down," centering power at the store level: "The burden is no longer on officers to tell managers what to do, but to support them in transforming the company."

The power shift has led GMs to think more broadly about Best Buy's business and to take a more active role in strategic issues. For example, at a recent town hall–style meeting, one manager suggested ideas for overhauling how delivery trucks are scheduled for unloading so that employees could be more available on the sales floor when they are needed. The manager's ideas have been widely implemented.

In addition, McGeehan says, "Officers know they can go to GMs for honest feedback that isn't clogged with political or operational minutiae."

Based on lessons learned during implementation of the pilot, Best Buy has fine-tuned the mentoring program to improve its effectiveness. "The pilot showed us that having officers visit stores during October through January was too narrow a window," says Steve Prather, who helped develop the program. "The holiday season is our game time." In a few cases, officers couldn't make their visits. Moreover, the time frame was inconvenient for managers. In future incarnations of the program, field and headquarters visits will take place throughout the year.

Some GMs also had difficulty seeing themselves as mentors to officers. Others had misperceptions about the program—assuming they'd have to "baby-sit" visiting officers or "race around cleaning up their stores," says Prather. Best Buy addressed these issues at its "Retail Road Show" in the spring by having pilot participants share stories with other officers and GMs about their experiences.

Best Buy's leaders view the reverse mentoring program as a work in progress. Their hope? To have one day a vast web of relationships through which the store managers' best ideas can flow into the corporate support center—and be put to wide use.

Reprint U0510B

The Fourfold Path to Figuring Out What Your Customers Really Want

● ● ●

Jim Billington

Ah, those inscrutable customers: you certainly can't live without 'em, but living *with* 'em isn't always a day at the beach. For instance, why do they say they'd buy your product and then go out and buy your competitor's? It wouldn't be so bad if the consequences weren't often disastrous. But as the graveyard of failed new-product launches attests, companies can't afford to approach purchase-intention surveys with equanimity. When customers don't do what they said they would, profits plummet and marketing managers fall on their swords.

Purchase-intention surveys are frequently used to predict sales of new products. But current research suggests what many managers have long known: all too often, the intent to purchase does not translate into an actual purchase. A recent issue of *Harvard Business Review* reported on a collaboration between Vicki Morwitz and Joel Steckel of New York University's Leonard N. Stern School of Business and Alok Gupta of First Manhattan Consulting Group, in which some 100 previously published studies, encompassing 200 products and 65,000 consumers, were analyzed. The finding: while consumers give accurate responses when asked whether they would try a product, they do not reliably predict their own long-term purchasing behavior for any type of product. Or, to put it in the more diplomatic language of the collaborators: "We were taken aback by how little predictive content there really was in those surveys."

But marketing has more strings on its predictive violin than just the purchase-intention survey. Today, businesses are able to construct elaborate personality profiles designed to predict how key customer groups will behave. And how clairvoyant *are* these rational-behavior models? Well, not very, at least according to William Massy, Ronald Frank, and Thomas Lodahl of Stanford, the University of Pennsylvania, and Cornell, respectively. In a recent issue of *American Demographics*, author David B. Wolfe cites the three academics' claim that personality traits can account for no more than 7% of purchasing behavior.

Reliance on rational-behavior models and allied tests

has caused some of the great marketing disasters in business history. The taste testing done before the launch of New Coke showed a clear preference for the new taste. But after the initial curiosity wore off, most Americans felt too much loyalty to classic Coke to switch, even if they preferred the taste of New Coke. Similarly, Kodak's "Advanta" camera garnered enthusiastic initial reviews because of its high-tech appeal. But aging baby boomers, the core group for whom the camera was positioned, had grown suspicious of the bells and whistles of high tech.

Why are customers so difficult to figure out? Conventional research assumes that people can accurately describe their needs and motivations. But as psychologist Bernard J. Baars writes in his book *In the Theater of Consciousness*, "Our inability to accurately report intentions and expectations may simply reflect the fact that they are not qualitatively conscious." Thus, when consumers predict that they will buy a product, they use their conscious minds, which only partially determine their actual behavior. Moreover, sometimes consumers predict what they think they *ought* to buy, rather than what they actually *will* purchase. Consider home exercise equipment: to the slightly overweight, the thought of buying it is virtuous and compelling—yet few end up making the purchase. The inevitable conclusion to be drawn here: people don't always behave rationally, and often tell others—focus group leaders in particular—what they want to hear.

So is market research no more reliable than reading tea

leaves? Not exactly. Nimble marketing minds have learned how to glean results-begetting insight into customer behavior despite the inherent unpredictability. It requires keen powers of observation, deep listening, and a nuanced appreciation for the various contexts in which customers may use products, as well as a Zen-like watchfulness.

"Watch what your customers do, not what they say."

That's the advice of Bob Lurie, CEO of Strategic Marketing Research and a director of The Monitor Company. Also weighing in on the subject of customer unpredictability are authors Susan M. O'Dell and Joan A. Pajunen. In *The Butterfly Customer* they describe consumers who "flit from bank to bank, credit card to credit card, service to service." Such customers move from one market segment to another, switching suppliers without compunction, and in general making a mockery of marketers' carefully crafted psychographic profiles. Sophisticated, and with access to as much product information as the experts, they have a heightened desire for specific products and services, but a dulled sense of brand loyalty. "Their first instinct is to try something new, something better, and something different," write O'Dell and Pajunen.

How do you deal with butterfly customers? First, you get close to them—and then you observe their behavior *before* listening carefully to their words. Kennametal, Inc., a billion-dollar metal-cutting tool manufacturer, sent 300 employees, representing a cross-section of the company, to the Bristol, Virginia, factory of its major customer, Dana Auto Parts. The reason? To see the conditions under which customers used their tools. The insights gleaned from this on-site scrutiny led to improvements not only in Kennametal's manufacturing operations, but in their new-product development and marketing as well.

When Microsoft began getting complaints from lawyers about Word 6.0, manager Eric LeVine went on the road to study how Word was being used in 35 different firms. In the process he learned how to distinguish installation problems from software defects and how to respond to each as needed.

In both these examples, recounted in Fred Wiersema's *Customer Intimacy*, the nuances of workers' responsibilities and the conditions of their work environment had to be experienced firsthand before their needs could be understood with sufficient richness. The logic of this is not difficult to grasp, and yet we can all think of at least a dozen products that seem to have been designed without any thought being given to the human beings using them. Even at that stage, when the ill-conceived product is foundering in the marketplace, companies could obtain valuable information simply by watching customers struggle with the benighted contraption.

But what's the point of watching butterfly customers interact with your product when they probably won't be your customers for long? Even the most quicksilver customers, say O'Dell and Pajunen, have value systems informing their purchasing decisions. Although cynical about advertising and product promises, they trust the advice of friends and assiduously investigate third-party sources. In other words, these customers may be much more willing to "switch than fight," but they nevertheless have a strong, latent desire to be loyal.

To retain "frequent switchers," O'Dell and Pajunen continue, companies must provide the very qualities that these customers lack. Show predictable, consistent service, and an absolute correspondence between what you promise and what you deliver. By doing so you can win back these fickle customers.

A recently published video toolkit from Harvard Business School Publishing Co., "Redesigning Product/Service Development," based on the writing and research of HBS professor David A. Garvin, offers helpful steps for honing your ability to interpret customer behavior and then translate it into product and service improvements. In one segment, L.L. Bean prepares to redesign one of its hunting boots by asking a customer to describe his hunting experiences in an open-ended, contextual way. This associative, wide-net approach to the questioning of users yields far richer and more specific product specifications than conventional methods. For example, a hunter's description of "wet, sweaty feet, prune skin" conveys more effectively to product designers the importance of boots that keep feet dry.

Using Customers' Experiences as a Guide to Better Products and Services

When L.L. Bean product managers wanted to design a new hunting boot, they asked the Center for Quality of Management in Cambridge, Massachusetts, to teach them a process called "concept engineering," which combines open-ended interviewing with affinity diagramming—a methodology developed by Jiro Kawakita to organize and distill ideas. The point of the process is to immerse yourself in your customers' experiences, derive a sense of their needs, and then translate those needs into better product or service designs.

Once you've identified a demographically diverse group of 16–20 experienced users of your product or service, solicit their opinions in an open-ended way. The goal is to get them to convey in depth their experiences: what happens and how they feel as they use your product or service and those of your competitors. Sample L.L. Bean questions included "What went through your mind when you purchased your last pair of hunting boots?" and "What features of other footwear or sporting products would you like to have in your current hunting footwear?" Such questions should be used in addition to—not as a substitute for—observing customers in their own setting as they use your product or service and those of your competitors. The following are examples of how L.L. Bean interpreted its user interviews.

(continued)

Arrange the quotations and descriptions you receive from users into clusters.	Write a summary statement for each cluster of quotations and translate them into product or service requirements.
• Walking through wet, swampy areas—feeling water seeping into my boots • Feeling my feet getting colder and colder while standing still • Putting on wet, cold boots in the morning—just miserable • Wet, sweaty feet, prune skin	**Summary Statement:** **Feet wet and cold** Product Requirements • Footwear keeps feet dry • Footwear keeps stationary hunter's feet warm
• Having to twist foot into the mud to get better traction • Slipping while sidestepping on a slope	**Summary Statement:** **Not enough traction** Product Requirements • Footwear provides maximum grip on slippery terrain • Footwear facilitates rapid movement over varied terrain

Source: "Working Smarter: Redesigning Product/Service Development," based on the writing and research of HBS professor David A. Garvin, copyright 1997, Harvard Business School Publishing.

Uncover customers' stories about your product.

The strongest customer segmentation schemes, notes Lurie, "are based on understanding what customers actually do, not what they say they do. Knowing your customer means knowing the stories that they tell themselves about your product."

For the last 30 years, Lurie continues, the advertising icon for Kellogg's Frosted Flakes in the U.S. has been an animated character, Tony the Tiger. Ads for Frosted Flakes showed Tony talking to the core target of the brand—kids. But the new ads show adults—their identities concealed—nervously confessing their love for Frosted Flakes. These ads have led to a significant increase in sales volume over the last four years, most of it coming from adults.

The secret? Kellogg figured out what went through the mind of a parent in the morning. Opening up the kitchen cabinet and looking at all the breakfast options—the Frosted Flakes beside the brans and the oatmeal—the adult thinks, "I like Frosted Flakes, but I can't have them—they're for kids. My kids would give me a hard time." In effect, the new ad acknowledges, and then interprets, this story that adult consumers tell themselves. It says, "Yes, we know you're telling yourself that it's not okay for an adult to have Frosted Flakes. But it *is* okay, because other adults do it."

Remember: context is king.

The team of Morwitz, Steckel, and Gupta concluded that the only purchase-intention surveys with even a moderately successful track record of predicting long-term buying behavior are those that ask specific questions and take into account the full context of the consumer. Thus, asking "How likely are you to buy a Ford?" yields a more definitive answer than asking "How likely are you to buy a car?" Better still is asking "Would you rather buy a Mustang or a Corvette?"

Lurie offers another segmentation example—the way American men buy cookies. Men buy cookies under two different sets of circumstances, he observes: either when preparing for an occasion, such as a poker game, or as a part of a weekly shopping ritual. The male shopper's behavior varies greatly depending on which of the two missions he is on. What remains constant is his desired experience—to make shopping fast.

Men do not like to grocery shop, says Lurie, and when they do, they consider it to be a chore. Often the weekly shopping is a task that has been assigned by the wife— the man knows he will have to report back. He may not feel empowered to change the list, but he can justify treating himself. Rather than bother with coupons, he will create "bargains" by purchasing larger quantities of a product. But when he is shopping for cookies for a poker game, he often goes to a convenience store and purchases several high-priced brands.

By thinking about the context in which men shop for cookies, a marketing manager might devise two very different strategies. The first would involve placing bulk cookies in grocery stores—close to the front of the aisles in full and easy view of the fast-moving male shopper. The second strategy would involve placing more expensive, smaller-sized cookie packages in convenience stores. It's the same customer you're trying to attract, but in two very different contexts.

Stay awake, grasshopper.

The complex motivations of human beings will always be the joy and the bane of a marketing manager's existence. But the bedrock of any consideration of what motivates consumers should be observation—in as realistic a setting as possible. The more alert you are to individual customers' behavior, the more you will know about their needs, and the needs of the groups they represent.

For Further Reading

The Butterfly Customer: Capturing the Loyalty of Today's Elusive Consumer by Susan M. O'Dell and Joan A. Pajunen (1997, John Wiley and Sons)

"The Consumer Doesn't Always Know Best" by Andrea Ovans (*Harvard Business Review,* May–June 1998)

Customer Intimacy: Pick Your Partners, Shape Your Culture, Win Together by Fred Wiersema (1998, Knowledge Exchange)

In the Theater of Consciousness: The Workspace of the Mind by Bernard J. Baars (1997, Oxford University Press)

"What Your Customers Can't Say" by David B. Wolfe (*American Demographics,* February 1998)

"Working Smarter: Redesigning Product/Service Development" a video toolkit based on the writing and research of HBS professor David A. Garvin (1997, Harvard Business School Publishing)

Reprint U9809B

Identifying Customer Segments

• • •

By identifying customer segments—groups of consumers with unique needs—you can generate more creative ideas for satisfying those needs through specific products, services, and processes. The articles in this section explain how to define customer segments based on particular criteria and how to use technology to further segment your customers.

In the selections that follow, you'll learn how to segment customers based on their profitability, their willingness to sing your company's praises to friends and family, their ability to drive business growth across product and service lines, and the emotional associations that particular offerings evoke for them. An additional article explains how to use the Web to gather information about specific customer segments.

Tuning In to the Voice of Your Customer

. . .

James Allen, Frederick F. Reichheld,
and Barney Hamilton

Call it the Dominance Trap: the larger a company's market share, the greater the risk it will take its customers for granted. As the money flows in, management begins confusing customer profitability with customer loyalty, never realizing that the most lucrative buyers may also be the angriest and most alienated. Worse, traditional market research may lead the firm to view customers as statistics. Managers can become so focused on the data that they stop hearing the real voices of their customers.

Financial software powerhouse Intuit briefly fell into this trap, despite a history of excellent customer service.

In 2001, its TurboTax program commanded 70% of the retail market for tax-preparation software and 83% of the online market. But then it began doing things that annoyed customers, such as upping the price of tech-support calls and limiting software licenses to one computer. Store-based retail growth flattened, and as Web-based tax preparation sites sprang up, online buyers started jumping ship. In 2003, TurboTax's share of the online market plummeted.

A recent Bain & Company survey reveals just how commonly companies misread the market. We surveyed 362 firms and found that 80% believed they delivered a "superior experience" to their customers. But when we asked customers about their own perceptions, we found that they rated only 8% of companies as truly delivering a superior experience. Clearly, it's easy for leading companies to assume they're keeping customers happy; it's quite another thing to achieve that kind of customer devotion.

So what sets the elite 8% apart? We found that they take a distinctively broad view of the customer experience. Unlike most companies, which reflexively turn to product or service design to improve customer satisfaction, the leaders pursue three imperatives simultaneously:

1. They **design the right offers and experiences** for the right customers.

2. They **deliver these propositions** by focusing the entire company on them with an emphasis on cross-functional collaboration.

3. They **develop their capabilities** to please customers again and again—by such means as revamping the planning process, training people in how to create new customer propositions, and establishing direct accountability for the customer experience.

Each of these "Three Ds" draws on and reinforces the others. Together, they transform the company into one that is continually led and informed by its customers' voices.

Designing the Right Propositions

Most large companies are adept at dividing customers into segments and designing value propositions for each one. But those that deliver a truly outstanding customer experience go about the design process in a unique way. In defining segments, they look not only at customers' relative profitability but also at their tendency to act as advocates for the company—to sing its praises to friends.

Customer advocacy can be summarized as a *Net Promoter Score*, calculated as the percentage of customers who would recommend a company (the promoters) minus the percentage that would urge friends to stay away (the detractors). Because such a simple measure is understandable to all parts of a company, it can serve to rally and coordinate the entire organization. The ultimate goal is to shift ever more customers into the high-profit, high-advocacy area.

Of course, the experiences that turn passive buyers into active promoters will vary by customer segment. What captivates one group may turn off another. In formulating segments, therefore, it's important to look beyond basic demographic and purchasing data to discern customers' attitudes and even personalities.

Vodafone offers a good example. The U.K.-based mobile phone company grew rapidly through acquisitions in the 1990s, becoming one of the leading mobile providers in the world. To ensure that its offerings could be effectively delivered to target customers in any country, it stopped categorizing its customers simply according to where they live, as most cellular providers do. Instead, it divided its immense marketplace into just a few, high-priority global segments: "young, active, fun" users, occasional users, and a handful of others.

It then developed targeted, experience-focused value propositions. The "young, active, fun" group was offered Vodafone live!, a state-of-the-art service that provides everything from games and pop-song ring tones to news, sports, and information. Occasional users were offered Vodafone Simply, which, as noted in the Vodafone Group's 2005 annual report, provided an "uncomplicated and straightforward mobile experience." Such clearly delineated service platforms allowed everyone in the organization to understand strategic priorities and focus on innovations that would better serve the segments.

In designing propositions for specific segments, leaders focus on the entire customer experience. They recognize that customers interact with different parts of the organization across a number of touchpoints, including purchase, service and support, upgrades, billing, and so on. A company can't turn its customers into satisfied, loyal advocates unless it takes their experiences at all these touchpoints into account. Design is thus closely tied to delivery from the very beginning. Planning focuses not only on the value propositions themselves but on all the steps that will be required to deliver the propositions to the appropriate segments.

Delivering Value to the Customer

The most brilliantly designed and insightful customer offerings can be rendered impotent by poor execution. To ensure effective delivery, the leaders must first create and motivate cross-functional teams—from marketing to supply chain management—to deliver their value propositions across the entire customer experience. Second, they must treat customer interaction as a precious resource. Data mining and customer relationship management (CRM) systems can be valuable for creating hypotheses, but the ultimate test of any company's delivery lies in what customers tell others. The best companies find ways to tune in to customers' voices every day.

One company that's particularly adept at listening to its customers and delivering what they want is Superquinn, the Irish grocery chain. Founder and President Feargal

Thinking Clearly About Customers

Which customers should you target? If you say "the most profitable ones," you're only half right. It's also important to attract buyers who will act as your company's growth advocates, encouraging others to buy from you. By assessing customer profitability *and* customer advocacy, you can tailor your strategies—and your investments—by segment:

- **High-profit promoters.** These are the customers you can't live without—your core. You want to design and deliver your offerings in a way that expands this group, and to target new buyers who share their characteristics.
- **High-profit detractors.** These customers, often as important as your "core," are sticking around because of inertia or because they feel trapped. They are profitable, attractive to your competition,

Quinn walks each of his stores' aisles every month, talking to consumers. Twice monthly, he invites 12 customers to join him for a two-hour roundtable discussion. He asks them about service levels, pricing, cleanliness, product quality, new product lines, recent displays and advertising promotions, and so on; he also asks what items they still buy from his competitors and why. Quinn uses what he learns to evaluate store managers and continually improve the company's strategy and its execution of that strategy.

and unlikely to suffer quietly. Losing them can dent your bottom line and your market share. You need to find out what's irking them and fix their problems fast.

- **Low-profit promoters.** These are diamonds in the rough—loyal customers whose current buying patterns leave money on the table. Tap into their advocacy by offering them additional products and services, but don't alienate them with heavy-handedness.
- **Low-profit detractors.** You can't please everyone. If there is no economically rational way to solve their problems, then help unhappy customers move to other providers.

We have found companies routinely surprised by which customers are high-profit promoters, how much potential for cross-sell exists among low-profit promoters, and how many detractors lurk in their portfolio.

For example, Quinn once learned that 25% of Superquinn shoppers were not buying from the stores' bakeries. When he made bakery managers and employees aware of this statistic and began tracking it, they came up with scores of creative ideas to build traffic. Customers soon were enticed to visit the bakery by the aroma of freshly made doughnuts; once there, they found baskets of warm wedges to sample. Today, more than 90% of customers buy at least one item from the bakery every week.

As Superquinn's experience suggests, people staffing

> ## Customer value propositions can never be static; they must be subject to regular innovation.

the front lines need to be well hired, well trained, and well treated if a company is going to deliver on its propositions.

Customer metrics serve an equally critical function: they allow companies to be sure their delivery continues to meet the needs of the target segments. But traditional metrics, focused on the performance of individual functions, aren't enough; measures have to be crafted to inspire cross-functional collaboration.

One example is Net Promoter Scores: improving them requires a concerted effort from the front line to the back office. Precise customer service objectives for specific customer interactions can also help to rally the troops. A bank might create a goal of phoning each new customer within one week of opening a checking account; a cable company, within a week of installing a line. Hitting such targets requires specific, coordinated contributions from customer support, marketing, channel management, and finance.

Leaders also find other, informal ways to let customers

tell them whether they're succeeding. Superquinn awards its customers "goof points" for pointing out anomalies such as an out-of-stock item, a dirty floor, or a checkout line longer than three people. The goof points provide discounts off future purchases.

Developing the Capabilities to Do It Again and Again

Customer value propositions can never be static; they must be subject to regular innovation. It's the same with delivery—every company must improve its performance quarter after quarter, year after year. Leaders in crafting the customer experience have established a number of capabilities to achieve this kind of systematic innovation and improvement. They include:

- Tools that aid customer-focused planning and execution. The integrated marketing plan developed by Vodafone, for instance, unambiguously puts customers at the top of the company's strategic priorities.

- Customer-based metrics and closed feedback loops that establish accountability. Enterprise Rent-A-Car tracks customer satisfaction with its rental experience on a five-point scale for every branch, and employees of branches that fall below the corporate average—getting top-box scores 80% of the time—are ineligible for promotion.

- Customer-focused management incentives. Net Promoter Scores, for example, are increasingly used in performance reviews.

Top-performing companies also create processes that seek direct, immediate customer feedback—not simply to ensure that things are going well but also to build in methods of systematic innovation and improvement. SAS Institute, a software company, creates a "SASware Ballot" every year, giving customers a chance to vote on a list of potential software improvements. EBay employees known as "pinks" monitor the company's message boards, quickly learning which issues, complaints, and concerns may need attention. American Express calls customers who don't quickly activate their new cards to find out if they're having problems.

Intuit turned around TurboTax's online market-share slide by, in part, institutionalizing its ability to constantly improve its offerings. The company's Consumer Tax Group, which had seen the biggest share decline, created a 6,000-member "Inner Circle" of customers who agreed to serve as a kind of ongoing, Web-based focus group.

They supplied basic demographic information, along with their response to the all-important question "How likely are you to recommend TurboTax to friends or colleagues?" They were then asked to explain their No. 1

priority for enhancing service in any aspect of the customer experience, including shopping, buying, installing, and using tech support.

A follow-up question let them prioritize a list of 10 suggestions made by other customers.

The Internet software that collects these ideas allows Intuit to segment customers into groups, such as promoters and detractors, according to their priorities and issues. Detractors wanted a new approach to tech support and customer service. Promoters ranked rebate programs as their top priority for improvement. Intuit probed for details: Where rebates were concerned, was it awkward proof-of-purchase requirements, slow turnaround times, or the amount of the rebate that most needed attention?

Thanks to these moves, the Consumer Tax Group was able to redesign its core TurboTax product, deliver it to the customer more effectively than ever, and maintain a mechanism for continually developing its related capabilities. Net Promoter Scores among both first-time users and veterans rose dramatically, and the company regained market share in Web-based channels and renewed share growth in stores.

It had escaped the dominance trap.

Reprint U0510C

What's the Cure for Customer Fatigue?

· · ·

Kirsten D. Sandberg

Companies spent $22 billion on customer relationship management (CRM) software last year, according to the Gartner Group, but just what did it buy them? The snazzy technology was supposed to make one-to-one interactions with customers a reality, but experts say all it has done is enable companies to disappoint their customers faster and more efficiently—anytime and anywhere. Customer loyalty hasn't increased. Companies still can't target their most profitable customers, and their data-mining and sales processes are just as convoluted as ever.

There's widespread agreement that customers are sick and tired—of the barrage of irrelevant products and services, the glut of marketing messages, the coddling and the patronizing, and the broken promises.

So what's the elixir that will reinvigorate them? Trying to change your customers is the wrong approach, say the marketing experts *Harvard Management Update* consulted—change your company instead. "When you really get down to what's driving customer fatigue," says Chris Goodman, CEO of Young & Rubicam 2.1 (the digital arm of the New York City–based advertising firm), "it's company fatigue—complacency about marketplace scenarios, the competitive frame, and the underlying wants and needs of the customer."

Sellers must reengage with customers, but not by "creating a communications campaign," cautions Jerry Michalski, president of the consulting firm Sociate, "because that approach has pretty much lost its credibility." Get out of the advertising mentality, which focuses on the messages your company is trying to get across to customers, and spend more time trying to discern what customers are trying to say to you.

Getting closer to customers starts with new ways of thinking about the people who buy your products and services. After that comes organizational realignment: changing people's jobs so they can develop an appreciation for how customers' needs for products and services are intertwined with their desires for certain types of experiences. For example, sometimes the exclusivity of a product—"I've got something very few others have"—is its primary attraction. When this motivation is at work, you're more likely to make customers genuinely happy not by chasing after them and carpet-bombing them with pitches but by teasing them into chasing after you.

But fine-tuning your offerings based on a deeper under-standing of customers' motivation isn't enough: trust-worthiness matters more than ever, and the only lasting cure for customer fatigue is delivering on your promises of providing real value.

Getting Past Customers as Data Points

"Companies have forgotten how to talk to people," says Michalski. As supply chains developed during the Indus-trial Revolution, sellers lost direct contact with the end users of their products. "Then the media revolution sud-denly separated everybody again," forcing them to inter-act through machines.

Today nearly everybody inside a company collects con-sumer data, but nobody has a complete understanding of the customer as a human being. Not surprisingly, companies' assessments of customers' needs and prefer-ences often lack imagination and nuance.

"If there's one word we have to kill, it's 'consumer,'" Michalski continues. It diminishes the richness of the interaction by viewing people as automatons that reflex-ively acquire and use goods and services in response to a particular economic itch. The term "customer," however, helps companies understand the buyer-seller relation-ship in terms of a broader exchange of information, ideas, and feelings.

Most organizational structures aren't set up to alert

employees to when they're not treating customers holistically—like human beings with a wide range of emotions and motivations that change over time, instead of as data points. As workforces have become more specialized, says Goodman, firms have tended to organize their marketing by brand, business unit, region, or sales channel, and not by relationship with the customer.

> If your customers are showing signs of fatigue, spice things up by playing to their desire for things that make other people envious.

As a result, many marketing departments, and even entire firms, have an increasingly fragmented view of customers. The remedy, Goodman suggests, is a "customer segment–driven approach" in which companies identify the "four or five critical segments that are going to drive their business across product and service lines."

For example, a financial services company might segment its customer base into the following categories: boomers who are downscaling, shifting to lower-paying but more emotionally rewarding jobs; boomers who are financially responsible for the care for their aging parents; parents saving for their children's education; and single women looking to buy a home. By assigning one group of service reps to each segment and training those reps to sell the company's entire line of products and services to that segment—instead of having reps for each product or service make separate contacts with each customer—the company acquires a richer view of the customer's needs and desires, a subtler understanding of how its brands fit into the customer's lifestyle and changing life circumstances compared to competing brands.

Selling an Experience

The better equipped your company is to view and treat your customers as whole human beings, the wider the range of opportunities it can envision for engaging in relationships with them. "Two hundred years ago, 97% of people lived or worked on farms," says James H. Gilmore, coauthor of *The Experience Economy*. "They made their own clothes, their own meals, their own tools." But eventually it became advantageous for them to pay others to do those things for them, either because they could make more money doing something else or because they wanted to spend the time satisfying some other human need. And therein lies a key to discovering new ways of making customers happy.

"The customer is whoever sends you a check," Gilmore

continues. "Everybody else could become a customer if you can envision offerings that they would pay you for." For example: creating opportunities for "direct contact, whether it's a physical or a virtual place, to spend time together." Such experiences can offer value by "restoring some of the relationships" destroyed by technological innovation.

Gilmore believes that "more of life should become a paid-for experience. Charge explicitly for the time people spend with you" at this place you've created, he recommends, and then "talk with them or observe their

Thinking Beyond Products and Services

Don't limit yourself to goods and services in your endeavor to uncover "the next wave of human need," says James H. Gilmore, coauthor of *The Experience Economy*—consider experiences, too. The following questions can help stimulate your thought:

- What are your customers, suppliers, employees, or even your competitors' customers making themselves that they don't want to make?
- What are they doing for themselves that they don't want to do?
- What are they experiencing that they'd rather not endure?
- What do they dream about making, doing, or experiencing?

behavior during that time." This is exactly what American Girl Place in Chicago does: it charges admission to a live, in-store theater production and to a fancy dining experience. It's more than a retail store, encouraging customers to spend time in a place themed around the

> Assign one group of service reps to each key customer segment that drives your business across product and service lines.

company's line of dolls from different eras of American history. The interaction is not about the customer's desire for a toy, says Gilmore. "It's about an experience that promotes child development and helps parents instill values in their children."

But a customer's desires aren't always so noble, notes Stephen Brown, professor of marketing research at the University of Ulster in Northern Ireland. "Customers aren't the paragons they're made out to be. Marketers should stop pandering to them. Treat 'em mean, keep 'em keen."

Companies need to understand that today's jaded customers see right through their manipulative ad campaigns. "We're dealing with very, very sophisticated customers," says Brown. His analysis of people's interpretations of advertisements reveals that even straightforward pitches get viewed with suspicion. Marketing must become equally sophisticated, he concludes; proceeding from "a deeper understanding of what people want than would ever emerge from the bowels of a data mine." Marketers must realize when customers want to be romanced, teased, even "tormented by deliciously insatiable desire." Play to such emotions, advises Gilmore. "Do the stratification and intentionally design offerings that will not appeal to everyone because not everyone will want or be able to afford them."

Or, if having their imaginations stirred is what customers really want, tantalize and torment them by creating offerings that change regularly or have an aura of mystery or unpredictability. The point here is that interpersonal relationships require a variety of experiences to sustain their vitality, and customer relationships are no exception. So if your customers are showing signs of fatigue, try spicing things up. After all, desire often increases with unattainability.

From Experience to Relationship: The Role of Trust

Crafting an array of experiences that deliver what they promise and satisfy customers' various desires isn't sufficient to create a real relationship. When a flaw developed in one of Intel's chips and the company did a poor job of acknowledging it and making it up to customers, the message behind its "Intel Inside" ad campaign—trust only those computers that have the Intel logo—started to sound hollow, and the company lost respect in its customers' eyes.

In a genuine relationship, customers see your company as trustworthy, which means that your marketing is backed up by authentic organizational behavior. "You can't just say, 'I'm trustworthy,'" says Michalski. "You can only behave that way" every day. And "if you screw up, then admit it." That's the only way you'll be able to maintain your trustworthiness. Such admissions are rarely easy to make, but in an increasingly transparent business climate, people will know when you slip up, and so the consequences of not admitting your mistakes grow ever more painful.

For Further Reading

The Experience Economy: Work Is Theater & Every Business a Stage by B. Joseph Pine II and James H. Gilmore (1999, Harvard Business School Press)

Reprint U0207C

Do You Really Know What to Do with Your Customer Data?

· · ·

Jean Ayers

With the advent of customer relationship management (CRM) in the late 1990s, companies came to believe that by using technology to tailor their offerings to individual consumers' needs, customer loyalty—and company profits—would skyrocket.

But in today's crowded marketplace, customer loyalty is more elusive than ever. A recent McKinsey study reveals that the annual churn in the wireless industry

> Try to close the gap between what individual customers settle for and what each wants exactly.

increased from 17% in 1995 to 32% in 2000. This trend holds true even in industries less susceptible to turnover. In core retail categories such as department stores, for instance, the top players' market share declined more than 10%.

Not surprisingly, many executives' faith in CRM has waned. In a 2001 Bain & Co. survey of the 25 most popular management tools, CRM was ranked near the bottom. In a follow-up study, 20% of the 451 senior executives polled said that their companies' CRM initiatives had failed to deliver profitable growth and had damaged long-term customer relationships.

Tempting as it may be to point the finger at your CRM technology, that won't help you reverse these worrisome trends. It's quite possible that the problem isn't with your CRM technology at all but with the way you are collecting and using your data, experts say. Although getting your CRM program in order is an essential component of achieving customer loyalty, there's much more that you need to do.

"Marketers need a good, thoughtful architecture to base their decisions on," says Harvard Business School marketing professor Gerald Zaltman. A more strategic approach to data mining can provide the foundation for that decision-making architecture. Below, advice on how to use information about the individual customer and the average customer in concert, and how to probe beneath customer preferences and behaviors to uncover the attitudes that provide a more solid understanding of customer loyalty.

Why You Need Both Individual and Aggregated Data

One-to-one marketing, a term coined by Don Peppers and Martha Rogers in their influential 1993 book, *The One to One Future,* focuses on share of customer: Using the insights about what makes your most loyal customers different to maximize the value of those relationships. By the end of the decade, many marketers had come to believe that the combination of mass customization techniques, sophisticated database software, and the Internet would enable them to actually deliver on the promise of customized offerings to each individual customer.

But that hasn't happened to the extent it should have, says James H. Gilmore, coauthor with B. Joseph Pine II of *The Experience Economy,* because "most practitioners have taken the concept of one-to-one marketing and bastardized it into CRM. They're using CRM tools to design better processes for a nonexistent 'average' customer, instead of customizing for individual customers."

He cites the example of a major hotel chain that asks guests to complete a multiple-question satisfaction survey via their room's TV set during their stay. When one guest answered "extremely dissatisfied" to all the questions, he was not treated any differently when he checked out. Why? Because his answers went straight to a central repository where they were aggregated with other customers' responses and used to measure overall market—not customer—satisfaction. A more effective approach would be to feed his answers directly to someone at the front desk who could respond immediately to his needs and create a better experience for him.

"A company's goal should be to learn more about what each customer needs so that it can close the *customer sacrifice gap*, which is the difference between what individual customers *settle for* and what each *wants exactly*," says Gilmore.

Steve Cunningham, director of customer listening at Cisco, agrees that it's vital to listen and respond to individual customer needs and preferences. But he believes you must also pay attention to the aggregate data—customer averages based on individual surveys.

"Let's say that based on the customer survey averages, you realize that your hotel is taking too long to check guests out," he says. "So you launch initiatives designed to reduce checkout time and prime your personnel to be sensitive to that issue. Despite these efforts, something goes wrong, and one morning the front desk manager sees a long line of guests queued up to check out. Because the survey averages have helped sensitize him to the importance of this issue, he knows he has to do something—for example, pull staff members off other jobs so they can help check people out, or offer free coffee to everyone who's standing in line."

Familiarity with the aggregated survey data, in other words, helps the manager tailor his response to individual customers.

Cisco relies on three layers of customer data to inform its efforts to improve customer satisfaction: The overall satisfaction survey that customers fill out annually; interviews with targeted customer segments, follow-on surveys, and sessions with corporate advisory boards that seek to identify an initiative that will address a problem hinted at in the overall relationship survey ("this is the 'digging and understanding' layer," says Cunningham); and, at the most granular level, records of each individual transaction that the company's technical support group has with a customer.

To illustrate how Cisco uses these three layers, Cunningham cites a hypothetical example. Assume that for a given year, the average score for product reliability has slipped a bit. Drilling down to the bottom two layers of data, Cisco discovers a problem with the power supply for its routers. It launches an initiative to solve this problem and identifies the number of spare power supply parts it sends out weekly as the measure it will use to track the progress. The transactional measure—the number of spare parts shipped weekly—may start to come down fairly soon after the initiative has been launched, but it may take a while before the change shows up on the annual relationship survey.

"You need both the aggregate and the transactional information," says Cunningham. "The survey data tells you about the overall health of your relationships with customers; it tells you which way the wind is blowing. It also helps prevent you from running after individual problems that may not be significant in the aggregate. The transactional data gives the detail behind the relationship." It helps you pinpoint specific issues that need to be addressed to boost overall customer satisfaction.

Digging Deeper

To boost customer satisfaction and, ultimately, customer loyalty, you have to do more than listen simultaneously to customer averages and to individual customers. You also have to look for what lies beneath the externals of customers' behavior (what they buy, how they buy, and when they buy). "Without capturing what is going on inside customers' minds and hearts, and integrating that information with the factual external experiences, the picture is incomplete," says Doug Grisaffe, chief research methodologist for Walker Information.

"CRM tools enable you to collect a lot of rich data about a customer's frequency and time of purchase, the size of her orders, and what she thinks of your company," says Harvard's Zaltman. That's necessary but not sufficient data: It doesn't tell you anything about "why customers do what they do, think what they think, and why they like or don't like your products. Getting that level of insight requires more intensive interactions with customers than CRM tools permit." It requires that you develop a "poetic insight into customers—a deep knowledge that enables you to intuit their answers to questions you haven't even asked them."

In one-on-one interviews with customers, Zaltman uses a process he describes as *metaphor elicitation* to get at the beliefs, emotions, intentions, and often unconscious attitudes that people have about a product or brand. As he explains in his recent book, *How Customers Think: Essential Insights into the Mind of the Market*, the information gleaned from these interviews as well as from surveys and observation is used to create a *consensus map*—an illustration of the particular bundles of constructs that customers have developed based on their experience and emotional connection with a product or brand.

A consensus map that Zaltman developed for General Motors reveals the richness of the metaphor elicitation approach. As expected, customers associated GM products with quality and competitive price. But there was more: Customers also linked GM with patriotic feelings. By buying GM cars, they saw themselves as not simply helping Americans keep their jobs, but as fulfilling a larger obligation that they felt toward their country.

Once you understand these often surprising bundles of associations, you can reinforce and sometimes alter them with the messages your company sends to consumers.

Based on the consensus map Zaltman produced, GM's domestic managers redesigned the customer experience at dealerships and added subtle cues in their advertising to make the idea of patriotism more salient. For GM's overseas managers, the task was more difficult but no less valuable for that. Realizing that GM products also produced patriotic associations among foreign purchasers, the overseas managers "found cues that underscored patriotic associations with the local country without pressing the American button," says Zaltman.

Reams of customer data are no guarantee that you'll be able to increase your most profitable customers' loyalty—you have to be sure that you're collecting the most relevant information. Listening for the attitudes that inform customers' behaviors and preferences, Zaltman maintains, gives you "a more solid basis on which to craft and implement strategies that will improve customer loyalty."

Reprint U0306D

Survey Your Customers— Electronically

• • •

In the digitized future, every company may utilize some form of so-called customer-management software, which collects and analyzes large amounts of data about and from customers. Meanwhile plenty of marketers have a more modest ambition: using the Web to measure customer satisfaction and gather customer feedback. Can it be done?

The short answer: in most cases, yes. You can do it yourself if you have a large enough number of e-mail addresses or a heavily trafficked Web site. Create a survey and send it out or post it. Alternatively, you can hire one

First Survey? Tips for Starting Out

A basic customer satisfaction survey, says research firm GuideStar Communications, should include:

> Overall rating questions such as how customers assess your company's products or customer service in general;

> Ratings by service dimensions and specific service factors (solving problems quickly, "interested in your comments and suggestions," etc.), plus tracking dimensions (service quality compared to a year ago); and

> Respondent demographics.

of the many vendors specializing in electronic surveying, some of which have already assembled sizable panels of ready respondents.

These purveyors are naturally quick to point out the advantages of online research. It's cheaper, they say, and quicker. You don't need large mailings (or huge banks of phone operators). It's less intrusive and more convenient for respondents, two factors that tend to boost response rates. It encourages franker answers to open-ended questions—and it's easier for researchers to know what to do with those comments. "You just pop that information in an e-mail to the appropriate manager," says Charles Colby, president of Rockbridge Associates.

Still, Colby and others acknowledge that non-Web companies have been slow to utilize online surveying. That's partly a legacy of the past: switching to any new survey method produces a different response pattern, so new data aren't directly comparable to data from previous years. But it also reflects uncertainty about how representative online polling can be. Plenty of people, after all, don't use the Internet much, either because it doesn't interest them or because they don't have access to it. Minorities, households with lower incomes, rural residents, and older people are all less likely to log on than the typical middle-class white American.

Online surveyors often discount the effects of this bias, arguing that they can correct for it with various statistical tools. Others aren't so sure. "There are a lot of people who claim you can use statistical weighting techniques to make up for [the bias]," says Howard Fienberg, a research analyst at Statistical Assessment Service. "But without those people being a part of it, you can't just tinker with the numbers so effectively. At some point in the future we might be able to do that . . . but at some point in the future all those people might be on the Internet."

While using the Web for general surveys may be problematic, it's a great tool for gathering information about specific groups. "What a lot of people come to us for is specialty research," says Janet Westergaard, founder of Esearch.com, an online research company. "They're really looking for a needle in a haystack. The beauty of this

> While using the Web for general surveys may be problematic, it's a great tool for gathering information about specific groups.

online stuff is we can send out a qualifying questionnaire to thousands or tens of thousands and find this very specific subject in a day, where if you're doing it over the telephone, it's going to take weeks and weeks."

Esearch client Eli Lilly, for example, found the Web valuable in tracking down people with obscure ailments for which the company is developing treatments. A client of the market research company Common Knowledge wanted a survey of people who used only a virtual bank. "We screened for people who have used an online bank and then separated people who use an online branch of their regular bank from people who were banking only with a non-brick-and-mortar bank," explains Common Knowledge president Steve Lavine. "The Internet was really the only way for us to do that."

Companies such as Esearch and Lieberman Research (which runs Opinionsite.com) get fast results because they don't do random surveys; instead, they have ready groups of respondents. These are people who have already given detailed demographic information to the company and have said they are willing to participate. Of course, most research companies have to offer participants an incentive, and incentives may eventually drive up the cost. Just as people have become less enchanted with phone surveys—some research companies report that responses to phone surveys are down 40%—so they may become less inclined to answer questions online.

Reprint U0004B

Communicating with Customers

. . .

It's not enough to better understand your customers' needs and segment customers based on their unique requirements. You must use your understanding to communicate more effectively with customers through a variety of means—including formal sales presentations, informal encounters, and even choices about in-store product displays. The articles in this section present helpful techniques for doing just that.

In the articles that follow, you'll find suggestions for adapting all manner of communications to meet universal consumers' needs—including interpersonal connection, the autonomy to make their own choices, and a sense of fitting in with their peers. You'll also discover strategies for avoiding an all-too-common pitfall: communicating with customers in ways that assume they are just like you.

Zeroing In on What Customers Really Want

· · ·

Douglas Smith

The days are gone when a salesperson could learn how to sell his product once and do it that way for the rest of his career. Today, getting the job done is as much about communication as it is about the product. But what do customers want to hear?

"Sales Effectiveness in World-Class Organizations," a new market research report by The Forum Corporation, concluded that "customers expect selling organizations to demonstrate understanding of the customer's business, goals, organization, customers, market, and competitors." In other words, the more completely you understand and meet your customer's needs, the more successful you will be in selling to her.

Motivate Action by Creating Competency, Autonomy, and Relatedness

Recent research on human motivation sheds light on what customers really want. Called self-determination theory, the research focuses on intrinsic motivation, the natural activity and curiosity of human beings to do something that provides inherent satisfaction in the activity itself. Paul Baard, of the Fordham University Graduate School of Business and consultant to sales organizations, shows how this works in sales presentations. Drawing on the work of psychologists Edward L. Deci and Richard M. Ryan of the University of Rochester, Baard argues that there are three innate psychological needs that must be met for a person to be intrinsically motivated to act—for example, to purchase a product or service. They are *competence*—to grow in knowledge or ability; *autonomy*—acting without feeling pressured or seduced; and *relatedness*—sensing being genuinely cared about.

The implications for salespeople: first, provide *useful* information related to the customer's needs. The key word here is useful; don't overload your customer with information. Second, respect her autonomy regarding the purchase decision. Don't use hoary car showroom tactics. Demonstrate how your proposal will benefit her and leave the driving to her. Third, establish and maintain a service-oriented relationship with your customer to create a feeling of relatedness or connectedness between her business needs and your ability to satisfy them. This is long-term stuff. Show her that she can count on you to deliver, time after time.

How do you reach this happy state? By communicating constantly with your customer. One of the primary ways to do that is through presentations. Unfortunately, presentations are among the most stress-filled, accident-prone activities businesspeople engage in. But sales presentation can be learned, just like any other skill. You may never learn to love it, but you *can* become good at it. Following are a few tips on how to carry out this vital and difficult task with elan.

Creating Relatedness

First and foremost, do your research.

If you do, you're on solid ground; if you don't, you're headed for quicksand. Ted Higgins, Forum's vice president, Sales and Service Market, and Danila Szekely, director of product marketing for the same group, emphasize the importance of up-front planning. A successful presenter is able to gather appropriate information about the customer, to understand the customer's business issues, and to synthesize them. As Higgins points out,

What Do You Do When the Curtain Goes Up?

"Most people would rather die a quick painless death than get up in front of an audience to speak," says Marjorie Burren, a principal of B&B Associates, a consulting firm specializing in business presentation and sales coaching. It uses a five-point exercise for getting you up in front of your audience looking like you are in control and comfortable:

- Walk up to the front with confidence.
- Plant your feet firmly beneath you, shoulder-width apart.
- Breath deeply.
- Look at your audience; make eye contact with several individuals.
- Smile and begin your presentation. Remember that your audience forms an impression of you before you start, so rehearse your entrance until it feels natural.

"Advance work for the sales presentation is what differentiates the top performers from the moderate performers. You've got to have an edge over your competition on what you bring to the table." A big part of that "edge" is thorough preparation. Szekely adds that top performers stay focused on the customer's issues, use the customer's language (not sales jargon), and are able to create a story with a beginning, middle, and end that links to results.

Organize your points with an approach that fits your material.

Are you selling a new software product? Most people use a descriptive approach—what the product is and what it does. Combine that with a needs/satisfaction approach—show a need within your client's company and demonstrate how your product will satisfy it—and you have a much stronger pitch.

Use an attention grabber in your opening—but make sure it relates to the topic.

It won't help your case to announce that Joe DiMaggio struck out only 369 times during his 13-year career if it doesn't relate to your customer's business needs.

Promoting Competence

Don't forget the visuals.

Clear expression and precise focus in presentations promote a sense of competence because they make the content easier to grasp. George Friedel, senior vice president and director of strategic sales for Parsons Brinckerhoff, Inc., one of the world's leading consulting engineering firms, has participated in more than 500 presentations over the past 25 years. His takeaway? He believes that "presentations are memorable for what the audience sees rather than what it hears." So, the graphics that support the presentation must be excellent and capable of standing alone to get the message across. The title of a slide should be a short sentence which contains the "feature," "verb," and "benefit." "Our Design Saves Money" is more effective than the typical title "Design Elements." To maintain clarity, many coaches and consultants use the 5x5 rule: in a bulleted slide, use only five lines of five words each. In this case, less is more.

Present your main points quickly as headlines.

Allow about 10 to 15 seconds per headline. Otherwise, you run the risk of losing your audience. Then, once you've stated your ideas in headline form, you can go on to fill in and add details. Substantiate your points with comparisons, analogy, statistics, or whatever proves the point best. For example, telling your customer that the software product you are selling will save her company time and money producing complex inventory reports may be true, but she is more likely to believe it if you can show that it did just that in a similar situation in another company.

Be precise in closing.

Write out your closing beforehand and rehearse it. Then you will say exactly what you want your customer to hear and you won't ramble.

Ensuring Autonomy

Talk to your audience like you would a neighbor.

Once you start speaking, you have between 30 and 60 seconds to win your audience. For example, initial eye contact is essential. Friedel of Parsons Brinckerhoff tells this story: "During one project rehearsal, the speaker refused to turn from the screen to face the audience. He kept reading each slide verbatim. Even when I covered the projector lens with my hand, he faced the screen and read the invisible slide. I called time out and took him into a separate room. He confessed, 'I haven't been this nervous since I asked my first date out in high school.' I suggested he think of this as talking to his neighbor in the backyard over a glass of beer. 'You wouldn't have used notes, would you?' He agreed, calmed down, and was one of the most effective speakers on the team." Imagine your presentation as a conversation with someone you know, a one-to-one with every person in the audience.

Use confident body language.

If you treat yourself with respect, the audience will reflect that feeling of respect and gain in automony. Uptight body language can ruin a good presentation. Paula Hill, director of the Business Leadership Center at the Cox School of Business of Southern Methodist University, remembers an executive vice president of a large financial consulting firm who, even though she knew her subject cold, was not an appealing presenter. Her whole body was tight and her voice was tense. She had a stern look, didn't smile, and clenched her fists. "Using videotape feedback, we worked on getting her to relax physically, make eye contact, smile some and use appropriate gestures. Once she saw what her clients saw, she was able to relax, her voice softened, and she became much more effective."

Putting it all together.

Making successful sales presentations involves combining the hard work of preparation with the insight that enables you to understand your audience. When it comes time to deliver, the winning presentation will be organized to maximize the customer's sense of competency, autonomy, and relatedness—and presented with confident, relaxed body language.

For Further Reading

Why We Do What We Do: Understanding Self-Motivation by Edward L. Deci and Richard Flaste (1996, Penguin Putnam Inc.)

The Sales Bible by Jeffrey H. Gitomer (1994, William Morrow Books)

Reprint C9909D

Are You Reaching Your Customers?

• • •

Richard Bierck

To appeal to retail customers you need to understand what makes them tick. What better way to do that than by studying actual consumer behavior?

A great deal of money is now being spent on quantifying and analyzing what shoppers do. This observational work is the bread and butter of Paco Underhill, a consultant whose market research firm, Envirosell, has been studying retail shopper behavior for 20 years.

Underhill shuns academic market research as being

too theoretical. Yet some of this research supports Underhill's commonsense findings. Such is the case with the work of Gerald Zaltman, a Harvard Business School marketing professor who has brought qualitative methods to what has been a field dominated by the quantitatively obsessed. While Underhill's work focuses on *what* shoppers do, Zaltman's deals with *why* they do what they do.

Both approaches hold myriad insights for manufacturers, retailers, marketers, and commercial developers. Businesspeople seeking to craft a more effective message to, and to get lucrative insights from, the shopping public would be well advised to listen to what Underhill and Zaltman have to say. Following are some of their communication secrets.

Examine the messages you're sending.

Are they the right ones for your customers? Are you getting them across? Many communication errors stem from a naïve belief among marketing people that they're necessarily trying to connect with people exactly like themselves. For example, many retailers overlook issues of nationality, language, ethnicity, and age.

"I was in Paris recently, and the cafes had menus printed in five languages," says Underhill. "But in South Florida, an area heavily populated by Hispanics, there are restaurants that don't have menus printed in Spanish." In Washington, D.C., there are drugstores that, "though they serve 100% African-American clientele, have hundreds of products for blondes."

In a labor market where youth seems to hold a premium, especially for marketing jobs, this notion is deadly for those trying to sell to an aging population of baby boomers. "Some of it is just learning manners," says Underhill. "If I go to a Web site that's hard to read because it's got funky type face, and I can't get service when I call, well, that's a problem." And many stores post signs with print far too small for many of their customers—especially those of advancing age—to read.

Don't rely heavily on focus groups.

"Focus groups tend to be like the law of the hammer," says Zaltman. "Teach a kid to hammer, and everything begins to look like a nail. You don't get a lot of depth in a focus group. People tend to say what they think they're supposed to say, rather than what they're actually thinking. And because there are eight to twelve people, there's just not enough time for each person to talk. The maximum number for effective interpersonal communication is three."

Instead, hire professional interviewers to probe typical customers' shopping motivations. Interviewers should be careful not to prompt the interviewees into saying what they want to hear—a common error that wreaks havoc with the results of customer surveys and interviews.

Reserve your best customer-communication efforts for the areas well inside the store.

Underhill has found that customers typically don't notice things placed just inside a retail outlet. The reason: this is a "transition zone" in which customers shift from their fast parking-lot pace to a slower shopping speed. As a result, much of what you may want to tell the customer in this area isn't getting across.

Some stores fill this area with barriers, such as low shelves of bargain merchandise that don't block customers' views of the rest of the store. But this can be risky. Customers sometimes just grab the bargains and leave without venturing into the higher-margin merchandise.

Communication itself sells products.

Underhill has found that retail environments that foster communication between couples or groups who shop together do more business. A pleasing environment with attractive lighting and décor not only makes an individual shopper linger, but it makes groups or pairs more reluctant to leave. So they stick around and talk about the items—a process that leads to more purchases.

Understand that shoppers are on a mental journey.

"Most of store managers' attention is on what happens between the aisle and the register, and that's where so much money is spent on research and package design," says Zaltman. "That's important, but there's a much longer journey for which the store is just a way point."

For example, he says, when a person is shopping for luggage, he's thinking about the vacation he's taking the luggage on. "He's thinking about clean clothes, getting the car ready, the whole trip, and all of these things cast a shadow on the luggage purchase. But these origins are often ignored."

Zaltman believes that the emotions underlying a motivation to purchase can be unearthed by research that probes the images consumers associate with a product or commodity. His patented method of doing this, called the Zaltman Metaphor Elicitation Technique (ZMET), centers on having interview subjects select images that best reflect their state of mind concerning the item in question.

The images consumers select reflect a range of emo-

tions. "That's because all points on the shopping journey have both pleasure and pain," he says. "Pleasure and
pain exist close to one another, and one can be triggered
by the other. The checkout person could be unpleasant.
Or, he could do something nice that makes it a positive
experience for the shopper. But if the shopper comes
home with something for a child and the child hates it,
this good feeling can go out the window, and frustration
can become the governing perception."

Take time to extract meaning from data.

Too often, marketing people assume that the data's the
thing—that it tends to yield up significance on its face.
But often, this isn't the case. The data may tell you that
something is happening, but not necessarily why. Those
who make assumptions about why often miss the target.

"Oftentimes, people confuse having a lot of data with
having a deep understanding of their customers," says
Zaltman. "Another misconception is that it doesn't take
much time to understand what's going on."

Companies that have succeeded at probing the psyches
of their customers, he says, have "taken a lot of time to
extract meaning from the data. They understand that they
have to dig more deeply and think imaginatively. Most
managers don't want to devote this much time to thinking. But they would never go to a surgeon who approaches

his job the way they approach theirs, nor would they send their children to a school that has the same atmosphere as their company; it doesn't foster learning."

For Further Reading

Why We Buy: The Science of Shopping by Paco Underhill (2000, Touchstone)

Reprint C0012B

Connecting with Your Customers

• • •

What's the most effective way to communicate with your customers? It's a question that has puzzled salespeople since the first caveman sold a used, smoke-stained, vermin-infested cave to his next-door neighbor. Do you push for the short-term sales success? Do you look for a longer-term relationship? Do you cross-sell every product you can think of, or do you allow the customer to state her needs? What really works best? There are three distinct models.

Courteous, Manipulative, or Personalized Service?

To understand the models, take a simplified example—the lemonade stand. There are three of them, run by Jane, Jessica, and Judy. When you approach Jane for lemonade, she greets you with a friendly smile and chats about the weather and other low-involvement topics as she fills your order. Jane follows the model of the Courteous Communicator. Jessica, on the other hand, greets you with prepared patter. "How can I help you? You'd like some lemonade? Great. Are you aware of our Frequent Buyers' Program? For the low price of 75 cents a month, you can have lemonade every day the temperature exceeds 80°. Can I sign you up?" Jessica follows the Manipulative model.

Finally, Judy greets you with a real hello. She talks to you about your dietary needs. What would be best for you, the sugared or the sugar-free lemonade? Perhaps you're diabetic, or you're trying to lose weight? Judy has an appropriate, personalized program just for you. You leave feeling that you may have told your lemonade seller more than you wanted to, but that she really understands your specific lemonade needs. Judy is a purveyor of the Personalized Communication model.

Which of these three models fits your business? Which works the best? What are the underlying issues associated with each? The research yields some counterintuitive insights.

One of the challenges associated with retail selling is the consistency of the script with the nonverbal messages the retail sellers send out. If the verbal message and the nonverbal message are consistent, all three communication models work well. Some studies suggest the manipulative model yields the highest profits.

But when verbal and nonverbal messages are inconsistent, customers tend to believe only the nonverbal message. Thus, if the salesclerk has been trained to be polite but reveals underlying hostility toward his job with negative body language, the courteous model will not work. Similarly, the manipulative model will fall flat if the salesclerk is hostile or indifferent. Only the personalized model seems to be strong enough to enforce consistency between verbal and nonverbal messages, perhaps because the model typically involves a longer interaction and allows the clerk and the client to form a deeper relationship.

The most important verbal communications that salespeople make are the opener and the closer. That's because people tend to remember the first and last things they hear and see in an interaction. Courtesy during the initial greeting and a thank-you at the close are the most important verbal communications salespeople can make.

Courteous service can be strengthened with temporal, spatial, and verbal immediacy. Temporal immediacy means responding to the approaching customer rapidly.

One study showed, for example, that as soon as a customer approached within three feet of a teller's window, the teller had five seconds to respond in order to have the exchange interpreted as a courteous one.

> When verbal and nonverbal messages are inconsistent, customers tend to believe only the nonverbal message.

Spatial immediacy can be reinforced by moving close to the customer, according to the cultural norms of appropriate behavior. Verbal immediacy, on the other hand, is expressed by responding with expressions that deal directly with the customer's question, rather than avoiding it by saying, "that's not my department" or "I'm not the one you want." Subtle verbal differences can create real changes in perception. For example, to say "We need to work together on this problem," rather than "This problem needs looking at," yields a much more courteous interaction.

With the manipulative model, researchers have identified more than 15 methods of controlling the customer-salesperson exchange to yield the desired result. Promises, threats, moral appeals, positive esteem, negative esteem—

‥kes the whole range of human weaknesses. ‥to be liked, we don't want to miss out on deals, ‥nt to be seen as successful and "in"—and salespeo- ‥e have figured out how to take each of these needs and incorporate them into pitches. The research shows that most of these pitches follow a standard model: first create awareness, then interest, then desire (by any of the variety of human needs), and then action. First, in other words, you make your customer aware of the item. Next, you create interest in the customer's mind. Then, you link it to a desire. And finally, you move the customer to action.

The research shows that there are a number of nonverbal ways to manage the underlying emotions in this interchange. For instance, a study of cocktail servers showed that customers who were approached with broad smiles initially left more than twice as much in tips, on average, than customers who were greeted with minimal smiles.

Similarly, touching the customer's palm when change is returned or touching the customer's shoulder during the order-taking both increased tips by more than 10%. Getting closer to customers, or squatting down to match eye level, increased tips as well.

Overall, the personalized communication model seems to be the most effective. It also takes the most training and effort. And, like the other models, it can be undercut by the unacknowledged prejudices of the salespeople. The research in retail settings shows that fat people,

poorly dressed people, people dissimilar to the salespeople (in terms of sex, race, class, or age), and customers who are aggressive or antisocial all receive less
immediate, respectful, and courteous service than others.
Women tend to receive slower, though not necessarily
less courteous service than men. And people with physical disabilities receive better attention than those who
are not disabled. In all these cases, training can go a long
way toward eliminating the differences.

For Further Reading

*Communicating with Customers: Service Approaches, Ethics, and
Impact* by Wendy S. Zabava Ford (1998, Hampton Press)

Reprint C0005D

Beyond the Carrot and the Stick

New Alternatives for Influencing Customer Behavior

• • •

Frances Frei

Special offers, service fees, financing deals—these are all examples of how companies try to influence their customers' behavior from time to time. Historically, the two basic tools for doing this have been the carrot and the stick. But some companies are having success with a third strategy.

So-called normative approaches make use of peer pressure and other social controls—some of the oldest techniques around. They establish credibility by tapping into the collective power of a larger group. In the right circumstances they can produce remarkable results.

Understanding the Choices: Instrumental Versus Normative Controls

Carrots and sticks are known more formally as "instrumental" controls. A specific reward or punishment is applied to induce the desired behavior.

For example, if you keep a minimum balance, your local bank may waive its normal fees. The bank offers you this carrot because it benefits by using your balance to cover the cost of servicing your account. At the same time, the bank may charge a fee for each out-of-network ATM transaction. Since the bank incurs costs for each of these transactions, it uses the stick of a fee both to discourage such transactions and to help cover its costs if they are made.

But JetBlue, the upstart low-cost airline, took a normative rather than an instrumental approach when it realized that it needed to turn its planes around at the gate quickly in order to achieve the efficiency required for profitability.

Cabin cleaning is a key element in the turnaround process. JetBlue knew that its customers were generally enthusiastic about the airline, so it asked each customer

ier area before leaving the aircraft. There
er frequent-flier mileage bonuses for a clean
r fines for crumbs on the floor—JetBlue simply
customers that they could help keep fares low if
they would pitch in.

Customers responded positively—even those who might
not have been eager to help didn't want to stick out as
shirkers. The company has been able to keep its costs
low and is profitable at a time when many airlines are
struggling to stay aloft.

Tapping into Community

Successful normative controls gain credibility from the
collective norms of a larger group. They reinforce that
credibility by building on the group's ongoing experiences. Several decades ago, when most businessmen
wore hats as a matter of course, it was considered impo-
lite not to remove your hat upon coming indoors. This
wasn't a law, it was just a social norm: Taking off your
hat was simply the proper thing to do. Compliance was
widespread, even though the only enforcement tool was
the scorn of others in the social group.

We are much less prone to such broad social controls
today (note the number of hats being worn indoors), but
in specific circumstances they can be as powerful as ever.

Now, however, we need a more explicit explanation of
the reasons for compliance and the benefits of doing so.

We also need to be part of a group that is willing to undertake enforcement of the norm.

To see how normative controls work, look at Shouldice Hospital in Toronto, which performs only hernia operations. Shouldice has a much higher success rate and is more profitable than other institutions that perform the same operation.

Part of the hospital's success can be tied to its particular medical practices: The facility is designed specifically for hernia patients, and it admits only patients who, aside from their hernia problems, are otherwise healthy. But that isn't the whole story.

At Shouldice, there is an understanding not only that the surgery is only one part of the process, but also that

> Customers must be able to see the consequences of complying with or ignoring the desired norms.

its success can be dramatically affected by what happens immediately before and after the surgery. Shouldice relies on its patient community—that is, its customers.

For example, each patient is expected to be a "hernia mentor" to other patients. Patients conduct the hospital's

ssions. They help one another with follow-
..ter the surgery. And the facility sponsors
..s among former patients.

..ich practices turn patients into a trusted peer group
..hat helps new arrivals understand what they need to
do to improve their procedures' chances of success. By
mobilizing the social power of this patient community,
Shouldice has increased compliance with best practices
and has dramatically improved the overall success rates
of hernia procedures.

Using Normative Controls
to Improve Quality

EBay, the online auction site, faced a quality control
predicament as it began to grow. Although its technology was capable of linking large numbers of buyers and
sellers around the world, eBay's future growth could be
threatened if customers found the experience unsatisfac-
tory. There was no way that eBay itself could police the
hundreds of thousands of transactions conducted on
the site without hindering the rapid flow of information
that characterizes the auction environment.

How, then, to ensure an environment in which people
would feel secure transacting business?

The solution was to let the buyers rate the sellers and
post that information on the site. The online community could set and enforce its own norms through the

rating process. Sellers gained greater confidence because they could rely on the experience of a broad range of their peers.

Meanwhile, buyers learned that there would be consequences for disappointing sellers. Thanks to this low-cost policing mechanism, the standards on eBay have become so high that some companies have found that they have to provide a higher level of customer service through their online channel than they do to their offline customers.

Zipcar serves as another example of the effectiveness of normative controls. This company provides urban

> Socially reinforced behaviors require some sort of connection between the individuals affected.

dwellers with access to private vehicles for periods as short as an hour or two through a fleet of vehicles shared by all members. The customer reserves a specific vehicle parked at a specific location in the city. (There are no central lots like those used by traditional rental car companies.)

Zipcar not only asks its customers to return the vehicle

on time, it also requests that they not smoke or bring pets in the car and that they leave the vehicle clean and with a full tank of gas. No Zipcar employee monitors each customer's use; in effect, the company relies on its customers to satisfy one another. In fact, according to one Zipcar official, "the vast majority—95% or more" of customers—understand the benefits of compliance and do so willingly.

Zipcar also engages in extensive community-building activities—from sending humorous newsletters to organizing its customers to make charitable food deliveries at the holidays—that help deepen the feelings of interdependence among customers. Given that 20% to 25% of the company's growth comes from customer referrals, the strategy seems to be working.

Even so, normative controls alone don't always work. Zipcar has instituted a late fee—to date, fewer than 5% of customers have had to pay one—and is considering raising it substantially for repeat offenders. A Zipcar spokesperson says, "No one thing works for everyone. For some people, a fine is a necessary enforcement tool."

When Do Normative Controls Work Best?

Based on these company examples, we can make a few inferences about the conditions under which normative controls are most effective.

Customers are looking to do things differently.

Each of the companies we have discussed here has an offering that appeals to customers looking for an alternative to more traditional-minded competitors. These customers may be more responsive to normative pressure if they feel it increases the new alternative's chances of success. The company's success reinforces the wisdom of the customer's choice, so the customer is willing to help the company.

There is a community of interdependent customers.

Socially reinforced behaviors require some sort of connection between the individuals affected. At JetBlue, the connection is physical—customers sit next to each other on the plane. At eBay, the connection is virtual. In both cases, however, customers can see the consequences of complying with or ignoring the desired norms—and they feel a natural inclination to act in ways that will garner the approval of their peers.

There is a high degree of trust between the company and the customer.

If Shouldice Hospital showed its patients a movie with actors demonstrating the right things to do after a hernia operation, there would be less credibility than there is when actual patients—peers with no possible ulterior motives—are the medium for transferring this knowledge.

Reprint U0303D

Enhancing Customer Loyalty

· · ·

One key benefit of getting to know your company's customers is the enhanced loyalty such understanding can foster. The articles in this section take a closer look at loyalty—including why it's important, how to measure it, and how to enhance it.

In the pages that follow, you'll find strategies for measuring the lifetime value of a loyal customer and turning first-time buyers into repeat business. Additional articles explain how to identify and address the reasons behind customer defections, as well as how to use customer relationship management methods and technologies to further enhance loyalty.

Do You Know How Much Your Customers Are Really Worth to You?

• • •

Uta Werner

In recent years, managers have been urged to gauge the lifetime value of each and every customer. There's good reason to do so. Examples abound of companies that overspend to acquire or retain less profitable or even unprofitable customers while skimping on more profitable ones.

If a company truly understood each customer's lifetime value, it could maximize its own value by boosting the number, scope, and duration of value-creating customer relationships and minimizing the value-destroying ones.

To measure customer lifetime value, managers must determine how much revenue each customer will generate in the future and subtract the expected costs of

> CPV quantifies the full economic value of a related product and service bundle over the time it is used by a typical customer.

acquiring, serving, and keeping each customer. In reality, however, very few companies can measure customer lifetime value. The barriers have to do with how companies are organized, how they make decisions, and how they track information.

Still, there are ways to better understand the intrinsic value of customers that circumvent these hurdles. While they surely aren't as precise as customer lifetime value, they nonetheless can provide powerful insights and help management make better, more customer-focused decisions.

In this article, we propose such an approach. We call it *customer placement value*, or CPV. As we will show, it can be a pragmatic compromise, generating much of the benefit of customer lifetime value with significantly reduced complexity. In addition, it can be a stepping stone to measuring and managing customer lifetime value in the future.

A New Way to Gauge Customer Value

Given the difficulty of measuring customer lifetime value, what is one supposed to do? Many companies revert back to single-period (monthly, quarterly, or annual) measurement of profitability by product or geography. The problem with this approach is that even the best single-period profitability measures cannot capture the full value contribution of a product to a company.

Consider a leading U.S.-based supplier of diagnostic medical devices. Typically, the company sells equipment such as blood analyzers to hospitals, along with testing reagents, calibration fluids, repair services, and other offerings related to the device.

The device itself typically would be sold at an aggressive price since the purchase is a major capital expense for the hospital and a highly sought after prize for device manufacturers interested in winning the business.

Looking strictly at the profitability of the analyzer in the year it was sold to the hospital is misleading since it does not capture the revenue and profitability streams of related products and services triggered by the sale of the analyzer.

When thinking through alternative strategies for the blood-analyzer business (including R&D investments in new analyzer models, pricing strategies, and allocation of sales and marketing resources), managers are likely to make suboptimal decisions because they don't take into account the likely streams of related products and services.

How CPV Changed One Company's Business Model

Using the CPV measurement process, the medical-device company described in this article created a clearer picture of how much money it was making from each customer. The results were surprising. A top-tier review revealed that large analyzers generated economic profit over the time they were in use, but small blood analyzers failed to create enough postsale margin to make up for their loss at the time of sale.

Going one level deeper, the manufacturer sub-segmented its customer base of small analyzers along a number of dimensions, including how the analyzer was used in the hospital environment. Here, managers realized that a small analyzer could be very profitable when used for more expensive, nonstandard blood tests (e.g.,

Measure the Customer's Value over the Product's Lifetime

By quantifying the full economic value of a related product and service bundle over the time it is used by a typical customer, the CPV approach helps avoid potential pitfalls like those the medical-device company faced. So, for example, the approach would measure the full profitability of a car, a photocopier, a razor, or a credit card to the company while the customer is using it and before

those typically performed on a small number of patients with rare diseases) due to the high profitability of esoteric test reagents.

These findings led to significant changes in the way the company managed the small analyzer business. It looked at a range of new strategies for smaller equipment, including:

- Different pricing plans for the integrated analyzer/product/service bundle
- Outsourcing manufacturing to reduce analyzer costs
- Lower-cost selling and distribution approaches

Based on the data from this analysis, it decided to specialize in small analyzers for nonstandard testing environments and invest in the development of new reagents for rare diseases.

it is replaced. In the case of a car, it would capture related revenue and profit streams of maintenance services, warranties, parts, and so on.

Developing an accurate measure of the multiyear contributions of a related product and service bundle for an average customer can be a helpful supplement to the single-year profitability typically tracked for a product or product category.

CPV provides a glimpse of the economics of an important portion of the company's relationship with a customer and helps managers begin the critical shift from a product-centered to a customer-centered organization.

How to Put CPV to Work

Companies follow a three-step process to measure CPV:

1. Measure user profiles.
   Measure the typical user profiles of one or more customers:

   • What is the initial "main" purchase?

   • Which related products and services are acquired over time?

2. Gather data.
   Gather economic profitability information—including net pricing, fully loaded costs, and a

charge for the capital used—for the main purchase and all related products and services.

3. Create a timeline.
   Combine the customer usage profile(s) and the financial information into a timeline of economic profits. Discounting this profit stream at the cost of capital yields the customer placement value. If the number is positive, the customer placement creates value to the company.

Realizing the Goal

When an organization becomes proficient with the CPV approach, it will have taken a major step toward measuring and managing full customer lifetime value. The journey toward this destination consists of three remaining steps:

1. Instead of calculating CPV for a hypothetical "typical" customer, measure the actual profitability of real individual customers until you have a CPV for every customer you serve.

2. Track CPV for a broader range of products and services than the initially assumed set of "related" products and services. This way, a customer's CPV eventually considers everything the customer buys from your company.

3. Look at the economics over increasingly longer
   time periods.

As with any practical approach, CPV has its limita-
tions. But when compared with the daunting task of
gauging customer lifetime value, it provides a powerful
and less painful entry point into customer-centric management with a clear road map to the Holy Grail.

Reprint U0408D

Five Questions About...
Customer Loyalty
with Jill Griffin

• • •

The longer customers stay with a company, the more valuable they tend to become. But getting them to stay can be problematic; customer defection is more likely to occur just after the first purchase than at any other time. How can companies turn first-time buyers into repeat business? *Harvard Management Update* asked consultant Jill Griffin, who has helped companies such as Dell Computer, Deloitte & Touche, Advanced Micro Devices, and Subway Corporation.

1. Why are companies particularly vulnerable to customer defection after winning new accounts?

First-time buyers are best thought of as triers: they're looking for confirmation that their buying decision was wise, particularly if the decision was a big, expensive one. If they experience any problems in postpurchase service— e.g., a missing product part or a service delivered too late— they'll regret their decision and won't likely do business with you again. Defection becomes even easier if customers still have a relationship with a former supplier and can easily return to that company.

2. How can customer loyalty be cultivated after that initial sale?

You need to track every step at which the company "touches" each customer—not only receipt and fulfillment of an order but also billing, returns, and postsale service. Managers need to imagine each touch point from the customer's perspective and ask themselves, "How can we coordinate these points to deliver a seamless experience?" When customers experience all their contacts with your company as seamless, they feel appreciated and reassured. And as customers have grown savvier about their value to your company, they've begun expecting more of these psychic rewards.

3. Does the array of purchasing channels available today offer new opportunities to build customer loyalty?

It sure does. Recent research shows that the more channels—for example, toll-free phone numbers, Web sites, and stores—that customers use to buy from a particular company, the more loyal they'll be. I advise companies to create cross-functional teams whose members think about what it's like to use the different channels from the customer's viewpoint. Together, these insights provide the "big picture" of the customer's total experience and help team members generate ideas for constantly improving that experience.

Channel coordination also provides opportunities to continually monitor and evaluate customers' experiences. For example, firms can take cross-sectional surveys of Web site customers' ratings of the company's service levels. They can conduct focus groups with store visitors, send an immediate thank-you letter to new buyers, and phone new accounts a month after the initial sale to ask how things are going.

4. Do frequent follow-up contacts with customers risk annoying them?

Definitely. Though systematic follow-up is essential, you need to make sure you are adding value with every contact.

You need to show customers that you truly value the fact that they are giving you a few moments of attention. For instance, suppose you're an automobile salesperson and you're sending a new customer a follow-up thank-you note. You might enclose an article about road safety, with a note saying, "Thought you might find this interesting." Or you could include a coupon for a free car wash, or a list of tips about car care. Your goal is to provide something that makes the customer feel glad that they took the time to speak with you on the phone or open and read your letter.

5. What do buyers value most about their relationships with companies?

They value reliability—you provide what you promised. They also value responsiveness—you're willing to help them, and you provide prompt service. But new technologies have shifted consumers' perceptions about what responsiveness looks like. Companies have to constantly assess these perceptions—and then exceed them. For example, if a 10-day turnaround for delivery of a product is the standard in your industry, evaluate whether a seven-day turnaround could drive greater loyalty.

But don't try to demonstrate unrivaled responsiveness on every front. Focus on what research shows matters most to customers. For instance, if you're a roadside-assistance company, your customers are going to care most about how quickly you send a tow truck out to them after they call your help line. They'll likely care less that the paper work is expedited within 24 hours. You need to decide where responsiveness is most critical in your business, then focus on improving it in those areas.

Reprint U0311D

Five Keys to Keeping Your Best Customers

• • •

Jim Billington

What's the most valuable asset of any business? In the past three or four years, it has begun to dawn on some companies that the answer may not be employees, brands, facilities, or anything else on the balance sheet, but instead, their loyal customers. This realization in part reflects the fact that in many industries, particularly manufacturing, new customers seem increasingly hard to come by. But it also derives from a growing body of work by scholars, consultants, and practitioners that has consistently demonstrated how a relatively small percentage of a company's customers often accounts for a large proportion of its profits.

As a result, customer retention—the art and science of keeping your best customers and selling more to them—has become a hot topic. Fueling interest in the subject is the perception in many quarters that the job is getting progressively tougher. Customers, including loyal ones, keep asking for more: higher quality *and* lower prices, levels of service no one would have thought possible a few years back. What's more, these days even customers who say they're satisfied frequently don't act that way. A multi-industry study by consultant Frederick Reichheld found that between 65% and 85% of customers who chose a new supplier professed themselves satisfied or very satisfied with their old supplier. What you have to achieve today, apparently, is utter and complete satisfaction. But this pays off big. In the late 1980s, in a move that helped kindle early interest in customer satisfaction and retention, Xerox made known its findings that totally satisfied customers were six times more likely to repurchase Xerox products than merely satisfied customers.

After combing through the literature on customer retention and talking to some of the experts, we've found that five themes weave through their work, and one overarching architectural principle: All the authorities emphasize learning, or, to be more accurate and slightly trendy about it, continuous learning, as the key to keeping customers—learning about individuals rather than markets, particular needs rather than average trends. Ever renewed learning, the experts say, will enable you to adapt to the ever evolving needs and desires of customers. Use the five themes that follow as a way to begin organizing this learning.

Identify Core Customers

If you fail to differentiate between your most valuable customers and all the others, you could end up trying to sell what one marketing manager calls a "Porsche breadtruck"—a product or service that cannot satisfy anyone because it tries to satisfy everyone.

The tendency to treat all customers alike may be particularly tempting if yours is a business like retailing, historically dominated by single-event transactions that don't lend themselves easily to developing an overall profile of the individual buyer. Dayton-Hudson, one of the world's biggest retailers, found its customer base eroding in the late 1980s, eaten away by competition from discounters and catalogue houses. When the company began to track the demographics and spending habits of its four million customers, it found to its surprise that only 2.5% of them accounted for 33% of its business. Dayton-Hudson had been treating these core customers the same as all the rest, focusing on discrete, one-off transactions rather than on enduring relationships.

According to Reichheld, core customers may be identified by finding the answers to three overlapping questions:

1. Which customers are the most profitable and the most loyal?

2. Which customers place the greatest value on what you offer?

3. Which of your customers are worth more to you than to your competitors?

In his book *The Loyalty Effect*, Reichheld offers several analytic tools to help estimate the value of each customer segment over the life-cycle of a company's relationship with that segment. He has isolated six components that go into quantifying the value of loyalty: the cost of acquiring a particular customer, the base profit that can be expected from him, the revenue growth you can anticipate from the relationship, any cost savings that may accrue from serving him, referrals he may provide, and the price premium that a first-class relationship may allow you to charge.

Reichheld warns that because accounting systems typically record transactions rather than relationships, you can't expect these numbers to be waiting on your desk on Monday morning. Obtaining them requires careful analysis. How, for instance, do you quantify the value of referrals? This is a tough question, but worth tackling, for besides helping you identify your core customers, the analysis can tell you a great deal about the key drivers of profitability in your industry. In automobile service, for example, referrals are critical, while in wholesale distribution the ability to achieve cost savings drives long-term profitability.

Calculating the value of a customer over the entire course of your dealings with him clearly points up the payoff from a long-term relationship with the right customer. In some industries, Reichheld found, a 5% increase in customer retention translates into a 50% growth in profits.

With the analysis in hand, you can select the customers you wish to serve. Some of the experts suggest that in doing this triage you should look beyond the quantifiable benefits from the relationship. Fred Wiersema, author of *Customer Intimacy: Pick Your Partners, Shape Your Culture, Win Together*, emphasizes the importance of outlook—yours and his—and of a good cultural fit. Consultant Wiersema cites the example of Caliber Logistics, a leader in roadway tracking systems. The company carefully selects customers who value outsourcing, have an entrepreneurial corporate culture, and are willing to share risks.

Identifying and paying attention to your core customers does not mean that all the others fall by the wayside, or that you are permanently limited to just that core group. Dayton-Hudson began a program to encourage loyalty on the part of its key customers, and in the process taught its employees the value of long-term relationships. One upshot was that the retailer attracted more core customers.

Measure What Matters

The experts all agree that the critical test of loyalty is, somewhat self-evidently, the decision to repurchase. Unfortunately, measures of customer satisfaction and market share often show a weak correlation to repurchase behavior. Indeed, these indicators sometimes mislead by building a false sense of security.

Standard measures of customer satisfaction have at least three problems. First, they only reflect past actions, not changing needs. Second, they don't really predict the decision to repurchase; unless a customer indicates that utter and complete satisfaction, you can't assume his loyalty. Third, they treat customers as a collective, not as individuals. Says Joseph Pine, author of *Mass Customization:* "Measuring customer satisfaction in the usual ways is really taking the measure of market satisfaction. You are collecting data about individual customers and then aggregating them into one number. An average, even a segmented one, tells you nothing about individual customers."

Another indicator that may mislead is a lack of complaints registered by customers. In his *Customer Retention: An Integrated Approach for Keeping Your Best Customers,* Michael W. Lowenstein describes the "complaint iceberg":

If you look only at formal complaints—the tip of the iceberg—you will miss the vastly larger mass of unspoken discontent. What cracks your hull is what lies below the surface. Even market share, that favorite measure of competitive success, tells you nothing intrinsically about customer retention, the experts observe. Nor does it indicate how much business you might be doing with each customer if you were providing greater satisfaction.

To get at this information, and to accurately predict repurchase behavior, you need to measure what Pine calls customer share and customer sacrifice. Customer share is the proportion of a customer's total potential business that you have. The higher the customer share, the higher his investment in loyalty to you, and the higher the barriers to entry for your competitors.

The experience of Pioneer Hi-Bred International, long America's leading supplier of agricultural seed, shows what you can do with customer-share analysis. The company, which traditionally relied on farmers working for it to sell to other farmers, had never attempted systematically to collect customer information from its field representatives. After making this effort, Pioneer concluded that it could increase its relatively low customer share by building on the strong loyalty it had won in the seed business to sell farmers other services, such as satellite delivery of market and weather information through a system the company named Farmdayta. A focus on customer share rather than market share also led Pioneer to redistrict its sales territories, arranging them by relationships rather than by geography.

Sacrifice is what your customer must give up in order to do business with you, the gap between what he wants ideally and what you currently offer. Says Pine: "Customer sacrifice requires that you know exactly what you can do, then in collaboration with each customer measure what it is he truly wants, and then use the gap between the two to drive how you renew your capabilities so that over time you get closer and closer to what he wants. You can't figure out everything the customer wants the first time, but if you understand customer sacrifice, and strive to eliminate it, you will have customer loyalty."

Putting less emphasis on quantitative measures, Lowenstein highlights the need for hands-on—or more accurately, ears-at-the-ready—contact as critical to gaining an understanding of customer sacrifice. He builds on kaizen, the principle of continuous improvement that has worked so well in manufacturing, to construct a four-step "voice of the customer" approach. VOC, as he calls it, seeks to make listening to the customer an integral part of the corporate culture, in part by paying close attention to listening skills, in part by directing information to those in the organization who can best use it to make a difference.

Analyze Defections

Once you know which customers you want to keep, you must look hard at those from the core group who have left you to go elsewhere. Too often companies skip this step; marketing focuses on rosy opportunities, not on apparent defeats. But in those lost accounts, great lessons lie—including how to win them back.

To this end, Reichheld recommends "failure analysis teams," each headed by a senior manager, each member charged with interviewing 10 to 25 defectors. The teams should use the classic "5-why's" series of questions to drill down to the root causes of defection: Q: "Why did you stop using our product?" A: "I got a better deal from your competitor?" Q: "Why was his a better deal?" And so on. The answer to the last "why?" may be far different, and more revealing, than the answer to the first. When first asked, customers typically cite price as the reason for their defection, but often price is a proxy for other complaints.

The payoffs from failure analysis can be significant. In "Why Satisfied Customers Defect" (*Harvard Business Review*), HBS professors Thomas Jones and Earl Sasser told of one company that regained 30% of its lost customers by contacting them and listening attentively to their concerns.

Mass Customize

Joseph Pine has coined this phrase to describe the way in which even high-volume producers of goods and services are striving to gain loyalty by treating their customers as individuals. Levi-Strauss offers a rudimentary example with its "Personal Pair" jeans for women. While jeans have traditionally been sized along only two dimensions, waist and inseam, these jeans incorporate two additional measures, hip size and rise. Pine also cites the example of Andersen Windows, whose end-users—homeowners—can collaborate with distributors to configure their own windows, aided by a design tool named "The Window of Knowledge."

Or look at the way State Farm Insurance dealt with its customers in the aftermath of Hurricane Andrew. As Reichheld tells the tale, many Florida homes disintegrated because they had been constructed using substandard building practices. Too often, the companies that insured them paid the claims, then canceled the policies. By contrast, State Farm not only paid the claims and renewed its customers' policies, but also paid to have the homes brought up to code. Such customization may be one reason State Farm has earned the privilege of insuring one in five American households.

Customization can be—and in many cases, has to be—built into a company's business systems. Wiersema points to AutoZone, one of the nation's fastest growing retail companies, with over 1,200 outlets providing diagnostic tests, parts, and repair advice to car owners. Each outlet carries a selection of parts skewed toward the vehicles that dominate that market area. Moreover, any employee can instantly access the repair or sales history of any customer in any outlet. Thus the company uses inventory management to address a huge variety of needs, undergirding its ability to tailor its service to individual needs.

Learn to Meet Unspoken Needs

Almost every sales meeting these days shouts the need to exceed mere customer satisfaction in order to build loyalty. Speakers get worked up expounding the mysteries of champion service: How is it that Ritz Carlton can know which kind of cookies you prefer *after only one visit?* Others exhort their listeners to make customers into "raving fans." But underneath the hype, there is a truth. Customers want more than they ever have. Presented with more options, their wants have become, if anything, more specific.

Guff Muench, vice president of Distribution and Customer Support for Cummins Engine, sums up the new reality: "The foundation for the success of many industrial companies has been relationships. But in this era of ever expanding expectations, satisfaction does not translate into loyalty. You can do everything right as far as spoken needs go and still lose the customer. You must learn to satisfy unspoken needs, and go beyond expectations. This comes from understanding what makes relationships tick, and does not have to mean big programs. If you are in an industry filled with rudeness, then courtesy can be the edge."

While technology can greatly enhance the efficiency of learning on this front, it can also erect barriers to human contact, which all the experts say is vital. Long-term relationships are built between human beings, not databases.

Learning about the unspoken needs of the customer can happen only over time, and through the kind of "customer intimacy" that Wiersema recommends. Nurtured effectively, such intimacy will gradually blur traditional dividing lines between buyer and seller, and ease the sharp clash of interests or the only slightly submerged antipathy summed up in phrases like "Buyer beware." The wise supplier knows that the satisfaction, success, and even happiness of customers is integral to his own success.

For Further Reading

Customer Intimacy: Pick Your Partners, Shape Your Culture, Win Together by Fred Wiersema (1996, Knowledge Exchange)

Customer Retention: An Integrated Approach for Keeping Your Best Customers by Michael W. Lowenstein (1995, ASQC Quality Press)

The Loyalty Effect: The Hidden Force Behind Growth, Profits, and Lasting Value by Frederick Reichheld (1996, HBS Press)

The Customer Loyalty Video Series, from Harvard Business School Publishing (1995)

Mass Customization, by Joseph Pine (1993, HBS Press)

Reprint U9607A

A Crash Course in Customer Relationship Management

. . .

CRM. 1-to-1. More and more marketing experts these days advocate learning about individual buyers and tailoring products or services to suit their needs, an approach known generically as *customer-focused marketing*. Is it all just hype? The experience of N.V. Nutsbedrijf Westland, a Dutch reseller of natural gas, suggests there's more to it than that.

At first glance, gas is gas—when customers want a commodity, they all want pretty much the same thing. So commodity suppliers typically compete on price, with the usual deleterious effects on margins. But as author and consultant Don Peppers explains, N.V. Nutsbedrijf Westland analyzed its customer base and discovered that many clients were greenhouse operators. "'Tell us what you need in terms of temperature, humidity, and carbon dioxide levels,' the company told these customers, 'and we'll provide the entire indoor environment you require to run your greenhouses—as long as you buy the natural gas to operate those environments from us.'"

Of the many different monikers used to describe such customer-focused approaches, *customer relationship management* (CRM) is probably the most widespread. Despite the hype surrounding it, CRM really does represent a break with past marketing strategies.

The Industrial Revolution ushered in factory production and advances in transportation, thereby creating huge economies of scale. Product-focused marketing strategies capitalized on these scale economies, and allowed big companies to sell mass-produced goods and mass-delivered services to ever-larger numbers of people. Over time, however, competitors' offerings in many industries came to resemble one another. The commoditization of mass-produced goods and services made it difficult for a company to differentiate its wares and left it vulnerable to lower-price competition.

With the development of inexpensive, powerful computing technology, however, the situation began to change. Companies were now able to interact with

Which Buzzword Do You Prefer?

Customer relationship management (CRM) is probably the most common phrase used to describe the shift from product-focused marketing to a customer-focused approach. Its drawback, says author and consultant Don Peppers, is that "it's a computer-specific term" referring to a kind of software and is often understood as purely a technological system. Genuine CRM, Peppers continues, is a business process: "to do it right, you have to integrate the front office with the back-office functions."

But *one-to-one marketing*, the term made popular by Peppers and colleague Martha Rogers, has been found wanting by other experts. James L. Heskett of Harvard Business School believes that "many of the companies who say they practice one-to-one marketing are in practice acting as if they know what's best for their customers." Heskett prefers the term *permission marketing*, coined by Seth Godin, former vice president of direct marketing for Yahoo! and founder of Yoyodyne,

customers more cheaply and easily than ever before. They could learn more about who their customers were and what they wanted. Analyzing this data, marketers realized not only that some customers are more valuable than others but also that the most loyal customers make a disproportionate contribution to profitability. They also began learning how to tailor their wares to fit better with customers' needs and wants—particularly the needs and wants of the most profitable segment.

because it "implies a partnership between the customer and provider." Godin describes the difference this way: "There's a continuum that runs from strangers to friends to customers to loyal customers to former customers. One-to-one marketing is focused on turning customers into loyal customers, and on preventing them from becoming former customers. The big idea behind permission marketing is that this continuum begins *before* the person spends the first dollar. It's silly to ask strangers to become customers without spending the time to teach them, to gain their trust, and to have a mutually beneficial dialogue instead of a narcissistic monologue."

Other experts apply their own terms to the phenomenon: *customer intimacy* (Fred Wiersema), *real-time marketing* (Regis McKenna), *continuous relationship management* (McKinsey & Co.), *technology-enabled marketing* (Gartner Group), and *enterprise relationship management*. To a certain extent, Peppers acknowledges, all these labels represent "consultants' branded versions of toasted oats."

CRM: The Basics

That represents in a nutshell the four-step process that is the core of CRM. First, *identify* your customers. Second, *differentiate* them in terms of both their needs and their value to your company. Third, *interact* with them in ways that improve cost efficiency and the effectiveness of your interaction. As Peppers and coauthor Martha Rogers write in their book *The One to One Manager*, the interactions should produce "information that can help you strengthen and deepen your customer relationships."

The fourth and final step: *customize* some aspect of the products or services you offer that customer. Treat the customer differently based on what you have learned from your interaction. This helps you establish what Peppers and Rogers call a "learning relationship." Does the new offering meet the customer's needs better? What would she change about it? The insights you gain from this interaction, in turn, become fodder for your next product or service customization. Over time, it becomes easier and cheaper to serve this customer. Your offerings should meet her needs better and better, and the customer should reward you because she perceives greater value in the service you provide.

Over time. Those words crystallize the difference between CRM and traditional marketing approaches. Traditional product-focused marketing is "a zero-sum game," argues Peppers. "Customers and the marketers who sell to them are adversaries. As the marketer, I'm trying to engage in a transaction that produces the most possible revenue right now. There's no future to the relationship—there's just the current transaction."

CRM, by contrast, recognizes that keeping customers over the long term is the road to profitability. Says Seth Godin, author of *Permission Marketing* and founder of Yoyodyne, which creates online promotions and direct-mail campaigns: "Instead of trying to find new cus-

CRM Metrics

The lifetime value of the customer.

Some customers are worth more to your company than others, and this calculation helps you determine just how much more. The basics: multiply a customer's expected number of visits times the average amount of money spent per visit. Deduct your costs of acquiring and servicing that customer. Add in the value of accounts this customer refers to you, and discount the sum appropriately for the time period you're analyzing. (Detailed calculations can be found in the CD-ROM *Service Success*, available from Harvard Business School Publishing.) The underlying principle: customers are more valuable than what they spend in any given time period—and some customers are much more valuable.

Share of customer.

This is one of the key measures for companies practicing CRM. It asks what the strategic or potential value of a particular customer is over and above that customer's current estimated lifetime value. In other words, what's the opportunity for increasing the lifetime value by offering the customer more than you offer now? To calculate share of customer, just divide: if the current estimated lifetime value is $1,000 and estimated potential lifetime value is $10,000, your share of customer is 10%. Unfortunately, says Seth Godin, "most companies have *no idea* of the lifetime value of their customers, nor do they have a very clear idea of how much it costs them to acquire new ones."

The Technological Underpinnings of CRM

CRM techniques have always been around, but according to Don Peppers three specific technologies have made it possible (and economical) for companies to apply the tools to millions of customers at a time. The three:

Database technology—not simply storage capacity, but also the ability to analyze and map large amounts of data.

Interactivity—Web sites, call centers, and any other means by which a company can interact with its customers.

Mass customization technology, or computerized standardization, enabling a company to break products or services into modules or templates. For example, American Airlines allows its two million registered "AAdvantage" members to create personal travel profiles, then markets customized travel packages to them.

Together, these technologies make it possible for a company to engage in the core activities of CRM. Explains Peppers: "I now know who you are and what you want. You and I interact. Then I mass customize, tailoring the product or service I offer to meet your needs."

tomers for the products you've already got, you find new products for the customers you've already got."

"And once you do that," he continues, "everything in the company becomes different." Because CRM approaches marketing in a fundamentally different way, practitioners have developed different performance measures to track the success of their initiatives. But the differences go deeper than metrics, adds Peppers. Not only does CRM call for a different mindset—looking at customers as partners with particular problems you're trying to help them solve—it also requires far greater coordination of business functions than in the traditional, "siloed" mass-marketing paradigm. For CRM to be successful, production, information technology, and channel-management functions all need to be integrated. In short, a commitment to CRM entails an enterprise-wide shift in competitive strategy.

Can Everyone Use It?

Some companies are better positioned than others to adopt CRM. The best bets? "Financial companies and telecommunications companies," responds Philip Kotler, professor of international marketing at the Kellogg Graduate School of Management at Northwestern, "because they accumulate lots of data on each customer's buying patterns in the course of their business." James L. Heskett, UPS Foundation Professor of Business Logistics, emeritus, at Harvard Business School, believes that the quickest impact of CRM will be seen in business-to-business marketing, "mainly because of the payoff [in] productivity, speed, supply chain integration, better planning, lower inventories, and more efficient logistics."

Other kinds of businesses may not benefit. "Businesses

where the consumer is not in contact with the marketer," aren't logical candidates for CRM, says Godin. (An example: pre-deregulation utilities.) Neither are "businesses where the lifetime value of customers is low. Businesses with huge churn. Or businesses where location is critical to success." Kotler, after mentioning financial and telecom companies, remarks, "I am less sure that it pays for many other companies to collect great amounts of fresh data for the first time in order to move into mass customization."

Concludes Godin: "There are tons of businesses where CRM doesn't matter so much, but I challenge the idea of a 'commodity business.' There's no such thing." That's what N.V. Nutsbedrijf Westland has discovered; so may a host of other unlikely candidates.

For Further Reading

Customers.com: How to Create a Profitable Business Strategy for the Internet and Beyond by Patricia B. Seybold with Ronni T. Marshak (1998, Times Books/Random House)

The One to One Manager: Real-World Lessons in Customer Relationship Management by Don Peppers and Martha Rogers, Ph.D. (1999, Currency/Doubleday)

Permission Marketing: Turning Strangers into Friends, and Friends into Customers by Seth Godin (1999, Simon & Schuster)

The Service Profit Chain: How Leading Companies Link Profit and Growth to Loyalty, Satisfaction, and Value by James L. Heskett, W. Earl Sasser, Jr., and Leonard A. Schlesinger (1997, The Free Press)

Reprint U0003B

What Customer-Centric Really Means

Seven Key Insights

• • •

David Stauffer

Loyal customers are like the real fans of a football team, says Chip R. Bell, senior partner in the Dallas office of Performance Research Associates. Regular fans are "at every game, cheering the team on. But real fans do that and more. They paint their faces with the team colors and wear silly hats. They *love* the team."

Studies show that companies with customers whose affinity goes beyond loyalty to love can charge a 15% to

20% premium for their services, Bell continues. But simply being customer-responsive or customer-focused won't get you there. You've got to go beyond. To get everyone—not just the sales, marketing, and customer-service folks—thinking about customers' needs, and to give them the tools to solve customers' problems. Above all, you've got to be willing to relinquish much of the power you wielded in the old days of command-and-control. You don't have to be a senior VP at corporate headquarters to make use of the following examples of what customer-centrism isn't—and is. Unit-level managers will find these insights immediately actionable, too.

It goes beyond handling customer calls efficiently. It means addressing all customer issues fully and resolving them completely.

"Your people have to be given the tools and incentives they need to push past the presented problem and uncover needs," says customer-service consultant Grace Major, who heads Sigma Service Solutions. The customer's immediate problem—the product doesn't work, the invoice is wrong—is often just the tip of the iceberg. "But that's what most reps are trained to respond to," Major continues. "They hear a magic word, such as 'broken,' and interrupt the customer in mid-sentence." When reps are trained to listen carefully and ask follow-up questions, they can push past the presented problem to underlying needs. Result: less frequent callbacks and happier customers.

But reps won't take the time to listen if managers discourage the practice. If you assess their performance only on the number or brevity of calls handled, "you're encouraging them not to uncover needs and solve problems," Major notes. She advocates assessing performance using "a balanced scorecard of measures," including customer retention, revenue per customer, and rates of repeat calls and rework.

It's not just ensuring that your support departments regard front-line workers as their internal customers. It's ensuring that *everyone* adopts an external focus.

An "internal customer" approach helps ensure that support departments assign the highest priority to the needs of customer-contact employees. But such an approach can't guarantee that real customers' needs are being considered throughout the company—that kind of alignment requires an external focus. Just what does that mean? If, for example, you're selling a car, you need to think less in terms of its *features* (such tangible attributes as how much horsepower it has) and more in terms of its *advantages* (the reasons why the features are important) and *benefits* (what the features will do for customers)—that is, how the extra horsepower will improve the vehicle's safety by enabling you to accelerate more quickly when you're on the on ramp of a congested highway.

But front-line workers aren't the only ones who need to see things from the customer's perspective instead of the company's perspective, adds Major. All employees must have an external focus. "You probably don't think of parking lot attendants for a medical center as being on the front line," she observes, "but they are when a patient who uses a wheelchair asks how to get to the hospital two blocks away."

> **It involves more than telling your employees how to treat customers right. You've got to give employees the authority and tools to decide the right way to treat customers.**

In the digital age, a hierarchical gauntlet of review and approval takes too long. Your front-line people must be able to decide what to do on the spot. At Rosenbluth International, one of the world's largest corporate travel managers, CEO Hal F. Rosenbluth invests heavily in new technologies that can empower front-line workers. Res-

Monitor, the company's low-fare search system, keeps track of customers' airline reservations and alerts agents when fares lower than those originally booked become available. As a result, the travel agent's role has expanded from that of reservation facilitator and ticket processor to one of travel advocate and consultant.

It's not a matter of steering customers through your Web site or store just the way you envisioned. Customer-centrism means letting customers interact with your locations just the way they want.

"Stickiness," that much-lauded characteristic, means that people who visit your store or Web site want to hang around; as a result, they are more likely to buy—and to come back. But stickiness is a company-centric, not a customer-centric, concept, writes *Wall Street Journal* e-commerce columnist Thomas E. Weber. "It tempts people to view a business through the lens of steering customers to do something, rather than giving them what they want."

That sort of distinction can be subtle, "but it's a very important one," says Patricia B. Seybold, CEO of the Patricia Seybold Group, a consulting firm. "There are things customers *want* to do and things that you'd *like* customers to do." A company wants customers to maintain their investment portfolio on the company's Web site, buy a digital camera for that new PC, and sign up for premium customer-support service. But customers want a company to increase the value of their investments, help them purchase a digital camera before the weekend, and get their new printer to work with their old PC. Their needs had better be met, Seybold says, because now customers can switch to your competitors more easily than ever.

It's not just giving customers what they want, it's giving them what they *will* want.

In the past, a company could compete effectively by assessing consumer preferences through focus groups and test marketing and rolling out a new, improved product the next season. That doesn't work in today's hyper-competitive environment. "Ask customers what they want," former Apple Computer executive Guy Kawasaki writes in the *Harvard Business Review*, and the result is "me-too products that perpetually trail industry leaders."

Today, the imperative is to know what customers will want before they know they want it. Spanish fashion

Companies Old and New Get "Centric"

Well-established and upstart companies alike can learn to be customer-centric, writes Patricia B. Seybold in *The Customer Revolution*. Hewlett-Packard, founded in 1939, has reorganized into two "customer-facing" groups and three "product-generation" ones. It named top-level managers of "total customer experience" for both its consumer and business operations. It implemented a blended channel strategy that allows customers to switch back and forth at will from the Web to the phone, as well as to other media. And it restructured managers' bonuses to reflect their units' customer-experience scores.

Timbuk2 Designs, founded in 1993, makes customized messenger bags, backpacks, and other carrying equipment. "We're changing the balance of power from one where products were *pushed* onto the consumer to one where the consumer *pulls* exactly what he wants," says the San Francisco firm's VP, Jordan Reiss. Customers determine the direction of the company. "That means all of our business processes—not just manufacturing— conform to our [mass-customization] model, from the consumer all the way back to the textile mill."

retailer Inditex is a leading practitioner of such magic. The company's roving fashion consultants prowl the hangouts of target consumers—hip youngsters—and spot fashion trends before the people being observed realize they've created a fad. The consultants send their findings to the Inditex designers and production managers, who are linchpins in a supply chain that speeds new fashions to store racks in a total elapsed time of four weeks.

It's not organizing the company to serve customers. It's letting customers determine how you organize.

In the new age of almost limitless customer choice, you're in trouble if your customer-contact people have to say, "That's handled by another department. Please hold while I transfer you." Web strategy expert David Siegel explains it this way in an interview with *Fast Company* magazine: "If you really care about customers . . . then you have to reorganize your entire company around customers. A car company should have a division for commuters, a division for families, and a division for sports-driving enthusiasts. . . . Sure, you still need departments like engineering and HR, but the customer divisions should be the power players: They should be able to partner with anyone to get whatever the customer wants." Customer-led divisions, in other words, help you prevent tunnel vision—for example, when engineering or design decisions get made without the customer's perspective being taken into consideration.

Customer-centrism isn't just winning new customers from recommendations of current customers. It's about having customers say you should raise your prices.

Focus on gaining customers' love, Performance Research's Bell concludes, "and they will passionately reward you with their devotion, their advocacy, and their funds."

For Further Reading

The Customer Comes Second (and Other Secrets of Exceptional Service) by Hal F. Rosenbluth and Diane McFerrin Peters (1994, Quill)

Customer Love: Attracting and Keeping Customers for Life by Chip R. Bell (2000, Executive Excellence Publishing)

The Customer Revolution: How to Survive When Customers Are in Control by Patricia B. Seybold (2001, Crown Business)

Reprint U0108A